How to Facilitate Team Work Agreements

A Practical, 10-Step Process for Building a
Right-Minded Team That Works as One

Do No Harm.
Work As One.

By
Dan Hogan
Certified Master Facilitator

Books by Dan Hogan

Reason, Ego, & the Right-Minded Teamwork Myth*: The Philosophy and Process for Creating a Right-Minded Team That Works Together as One*

Right-Minded Teamwork in Any Team*: The Ultimate Team Building Method to Create a Team That Works as One*

How to Facilitate Team Work Agreements*: A Practical, 10-Step Process for Building a Right-Minded Team That Works as One*

How to Apply the Right Choice Model*:*
Create a Right-Minded Team That Works as One

7 Mindfulness Training Lessons*: Improve Teammates' Ability to Work as One with Right-Minded Thinking*

Right-Minded Teamwork*:*
9 Right Choices for Building a Team That Works as One

Design a Right-Minded, Team-Building Workshop*:*
12 Steps to Create a Team That Works as One

Achieve Your Organization's Strategic Plan*: Create a Right-Minded Team Management System to Ensure All Teams Work as One*

ISBN: 978-1-939585-06-6

Acknowledgments & Appreciations

To the thousands of teammates, team leaders,
and team-building facilitators with whom I've
worked with over the last 40 years,

Thank You

For being my teacher.

Collectively, we created this
awesome team-building program.

*Right-Minded Teamwork is a business-oriented,
psychological approach to team building where
acceptance, forgiveness, and adjustment
are teammate characteristics,
and customer satisfaction
is the team's result.*

In addition, there are several special people I want to joyfully acknowledge and thank for their contributions.

First and foremost, I want to convey my deep and heartfelt gratitude to our editor, Erin Leigh. Thanks to her superb editing and vital guidance, Right-Minded Teamwork is now much easier to understand and successfully integrate into your team. Thank you, Erin. The RMT book series would not have happened without you.
(To contact Erin, email erin@thechoice.life.)

Next, a giant thank you to the Ebook Launch team. Dane Low, our book cover designer, created exceptional cover designs for the Right-Minded Teamwork book series. Thank you for elevating Right-Minded Teamwork. (To reach Dane visit EbookLaunch.com.)

Another sincere thank you goes out to Cathi Bosco, our graphic artist, who renovated and modernized many of our Right-Minded Teamwork process models, graphics, and illustrations
(reach her at CathiBosco.com).
And I also want to thank the Media A-Team, who created the original and current versions of the Right Choice Model
(find them at Mediaateam.com).

Finally, I want to express my gratitude to Jackie D'Elia, our website and UX designer, who successfully modernized the RightMindedTeamwork.com website into an easy-to-use platform. Her work allows us to share the RMT books, models, and other resources and materials with the world. Thank you, Jackie.
(Contact Jackie at JackieDElia.com.)

CONTENTS

5 Elements of Right-Minded TEAMWORK

Psychological Goals
Achieve Emotionally-Intelligent Teammate Work Behavior

2

Business Goals
Achieve 100% Team Customer Satisfaction

1

Framework:
2 Goals
+
3 Methods
=
100% Team Customer Satisfaction

3

Work Agreements
Create and Follow Commitments

4

Operating System
Build an Effective & Efficient Operating System

5

Teammate
Strengthen Individual Performance

Let's go!
Apply the Three Workshop Implementation Plan to incorporate all 5 Elements

6 - 12 Month Continuous Improvement Plan

Preface

Welcome to Right-Minded Teamwork (RMT).

What is RMT?

Right-Minded Teamwork is an intelligent and empowering teamwork system that creates a *team that works together as one.*

Every one of us has the right to experience the magic that can happen when teammates work together as *one unified team.* Each of us can claim and exercise that right, starting right now, if we choose. That is why RMT is for everyone, everywhere, forever. And, through these pages, it is available to you.

Apply RMT, and you will improve your work processes and strengthen your relationships.

Apply RMT, and your team will achieve 100% customer satisfaction.

Apply RMT, and your team will *work together as one.*

You'll also do your part to make the world a better place for everyone, everywhere, forever.

Let's get started right now.

· · · · ·

It is an honor to introduce you to Right-Minded Teamwork's **Work Agreement** process. This real-world team-building method has improved the lives and teams of thousands of people worldwide.

Apply Work Agreements in your team, and you, too, will reap their benefits.

But first, let's talk about a few key RMT terms and concepts that will help you on your way.

What Is "Right" in Right-Minded Teamwork?

RMT has nothing to do with right-brain thinking or right-wing viewpoints.

It has everything to do with what your team, together, decides is "right." You and your teammates, collectively, define your Right-Minded attitudes and work behaviors.

The "right" way is the way you choose is right for your team.

So, how do you open up a team discussion about what is right or wrong? You collaboratively create and actively live team **Work Agreements.**

Work Agreements: What Are They?

A team without Work Agreements is like a complex machine without an operator's manual. If not actively maintained, performance will eventually degrade. Teammates might function at acceptable levels for a while, but without Work Agreements, they will eventually decline into separateness and egotistical self-interest.

A Work Agreement is a covenant, promise, or pledge that transforms dysfunctional and non-productive work behavior. It is not a ground rule. It is an emotionally mature promise based on collaboration and achieving customer satisfaction.

Emotionally mature and productive teammates create Work Agreements to guide them. They strive to sustain Right-Minded Teamwork because they have experienced the benefits of a unified team with shared interests and common goals.

In the book ***Right-Minded Teamwork in Any Team****: The Ultimate Team Building Method to Create a Team That Works as One,* you will find this definition of Right-Minded Teamwork:

> *Right-Minded Teamwork is a business-oriented, psychological approach to team building where **acceptance**, **forgiveness**, and **adjustment** are teammate characteristics, and 100% customer satisfaction is the team's result.*

When you apply RMT, your Work Agreements describe what acceptance, forgiveness, and adjustment look like **on your team**. They define your psychological approach to teamwork, or your team's Right-Minded thought system.

If you're curious about what a Work Agreement actually looks like, here's a sneak peek. You'll also find this Work Agreement and another real-world example later in this book, in *The Work Agreement Facilitation Process* section.

Behavioral Agreement – Communication

Team Choice: Intention Statement
1. Each teammate will communicate in a respectful way.

Clarifications / Conditions for Acceptance:

A. We will use good communication techniques that include appropriate body language and tone of voice, plus suitable words.
B. If we see or hear disrespect or we hear an inappropriate behind-the-back conversation, we own it and need to step in.
C. If someone unintentionally shows disrespect, we will give them the benefit of the doubt, let them know, and create a new way to interact going forward.
D. We will actively support team decisions in word, deed, and energy; we will use our decision-making protocol agreement for key decisions.
E. We will be on time for meetings.
F. We will ask, "May I interrupt you?"
G. We will use observable facts during disagreements and decision-making, and we will acknowledge when we are using assumptions.
H. We will understand each other's roles, ask for help if we need it, share relevant information and if helpful, give constructive feedback in private.
I. If someone continues to break this agreement, we will tell them that we will invite a third party to help if there is continued disagreement. If that doesn't solve the issues, we will all go to a higher authority for support and resolution.

In RMT's book ***Reason, Ego & the Right-Minded Teamwork Myth****: The Philosophy and Process for Creating a Right-Minded Team that Works Together as One,* you learned that you – the **Decision-Maker** – follow either Reason or Ego.

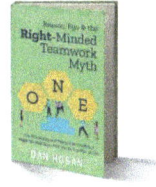

Reason encourages you and your teammates to create Work Agreements because Reason knows they will help you work together to achieve 100% customer satisfaction. Creating and following your Agreements means you are in charge of and in control of your collective Right Mind.

Ego, on the other hand, does not want you to make Work Agreements. Ego wants you to be a victim who blames others or a victimizer who attacks others.

Teammates who follow Reason succeed. They pull from their collective Right Mind to create Work Agreements. Then they intentionally choose to follow their Agreements instead of Ego. When teammates create and live their Work Agreements, they return to the **Unified Circle of Right-Minded Thinking.** In this space, it is easy to recover from difficult team situations.

EGO

DECISION MAKER

REASON

Work Agreements: How to Create Them

This book will teach you how to successfully facilitate Work Agreements. Everything you need to know to get started can be found here.

Strictly speaking, there is no one absolute right way to facilitate Work Agreement dialogues, but there are a number of fundamental principles for moving teammates into their collective Right Minds.

Those key principles are the 10 Steps covered in this book. Learn them, and you will succeed.

In the thirty-five years of my team-building career, I facilitated over 500 teams in varying states of conflict and dysfunction. Every team created some kind of Work Agreement and succeeded as a result.

Work Agreements work when teammates live them.

Since you have worked in teams, you know it is not a matter of *if* conflict will occur among teammates. It is a question of *when*. For that reason, it is far better to have Work Agreements in place before disagreements happen. Your existing Work Agreements will serve to mitigate and even make positive use of those clashes when they occur.

However, even if your team is already in conflict, it's still not - and will never be - too late to create and live Work Agreements.

In short, Work Agreements are created in team workshops where leaders and teammates openly discuss unresolved interpersonal or work process issues that are already hurting or have the potential to hurt team performance. These issues are addressed through team-wide Work Agreements.

Maybe you have already skimmed ahead and looked at the 10 Steps covered in this book. If so, it may feel like facilitating Work Agreements is too much, maybe more than your team needs. If that's the case, pause for a moment and consider the bigger picture.

The 10 Steps to facilitating and creating Work Agreements are logical and practical. When followed, Work Agreements are consistently effective. Your Right Mind already knows this to be true. It will only take facilitating your first two or three teams using the 10 Steps to confirm this truth for yourself.

As you practice, remember you will make mistakes, especially in the beginning. Don't give up. The long-lasting benefits you will bring to your teams will far outweigh any initial missteps.

In This Book

In the next section, you will learn how Work Agreements fit into Right-Minded Teamwork's 5 Elements model. Additionally, you will:

- see two real, successful team Work Agreements
- receive a three-workshop implementation plan, with the first workshop primarily focused on creating team Work Agreements
- learn how *Right Choice* will help you choose the right attitudes and behaviors for your team's Work Agreements.

After that, we'll explore the 10 Steps to creating Work Agreements.

Together, we'll walk through:
- a brief, **narrative explanation of how to create Work Agreements**, where we'll summarize each of the 10 Steps
- a **graphic illustration of the Work Agreements process** that illustrates the step-by-step process of transforming workshop flipcharts into a team Work Agreement,
- a **detailed explanation of the 10 Steps** with specific tips and techniques for successfully facilitating each one.

We'll also explore how to live and sustain your Work Agreements after your team-building workshop. And we'll share resources and templates to help you improve your facilitation skills.

Welcome to Your New Role: RMT Facilitator

Now that you have a clearer sense of the journey we'll be taking together through these pages, I want to take a moment to congratulate you on your new role. Incorporating Work Agreements into your team-building repertoire means **you are now a Right-Minded Teamwork Facilitator.**

As an RMT Facilitator, **your specialty is team transformations**.

Using RMT, you help to transform dysfunctional souls into healthy and functional teammates. You guide teammates to convert their mistakes into Right-Minded attitudes and behaviors. They express their deep and heartfelt gratitude for your facilitation efforts and results. Some even say you "saved them," continuing to seek your support for years to come.

Whether you're new to facilitation or continuing to build your team-building toolkit, add RMT to your practice today. There's no reason not to: All parts of Right-Minded Teamwork, including Work Agreements, are available for your use. There are no licensing or certification requirements.

My only request is that you accept Reason's wisdom on this path. With Reason's guidance, you can easily apply these methods to help your client teams create and sustain Right-Minded Teamwork.

My Special Support Function

It took countless workshops, a 35-year career in active team-building facilitation, and the collective wisdom of so many teammates and team leaders to conceptualize and build Right-Minded Teamwork into the robust model it is today.

Though I no longer facilitate actively, choosing to pass that torch on to the next generation of facilitators, I will always continue to promote Right-Minded Teamwork.

The reason for my continued passion is quite simple. I know, beyond a shadow of a doubt, that RMT and team Work Agreements are right for every team, everywhere, forever. If you use them, they *will* help make your client team(s) and the world a better place.

To make that happen, though, **your clients need you to show them and their teams the Right-Minded Teamwork way.**

As you lead them down the RMT path, remember: I am here to support you. So, reach out to me. Ask me questions. Let me get to know you so I can refer you to clients looking for an RMT Facilitator.

Also remember that even though you will undoubtedly help your client teams achieve an "early win," creating and sustaining Right-Minded Teamwork takes at least a year.

So, as you enter into the team-building process, stick with it for the long haul. Plan to stay with your team(s) for at least one to two years. Help them firmly establish RMT in their team. Give them the foundation they need to learn, grow, and succeed.

As you do, you will do your part to make the world a better place for everyone, everywhere, forever.

Let's get started now.

Dan Hogan

Work Agreements &
the RMT Process

The Right-Minded Teamwork framework includes 5 Elements. Two are goals, and three are methods to attain those goals.

Work Agreements are the third Element of Right-Minded Teamwork's 5 Elements model.

All 5 Elements work together to ensure a team achieves the business goal of 100% customer satisfaction, as follows:

1. Team **Business Goal**: Achieve 100% Customer Satisfaction

2. Team **Psychological Goal**: Commit to Right-Minded Thinking

3. Team **Work Agreements**: Create & Follow Commitments

4. **Team Operating System**: Make It Effective & Efficient

5. **Right-Minded Teammates**: Strengthen Individual Performance

5 Elements of Right-Minded TEAMWORK

Psychological Goals
Achieve Emotionally-Intelligent Teammate Work Behavior
2

Business Goals
Achieve 100% Team Customer Satisfaction
1

3
Work Agreements
Create and Follow Commitments

Framework:
2 Goals
+
3 Methods
=
100% Team Customer Satisfaction

4
Operating System
Build an Effective & Efficient Operating System

Let's go!
Apply the Three Workshop Implementation Plan to Incorporate all 5 Elements

5
Teammate
Strengthen Individual Performance

6 - 12 Month Continuous Improvement Plan

Copyright © 2019 Right-Minded Teamwork

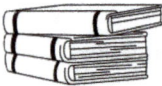

To Learn More...

For a more detailed description of RMT's 5 Elements framework and process, go to RightMindedTeamwork.com, and pick up your copy of ***Right-Minded Teamwork in Any Team***: *The Ultimate Team Building Method to Create a Team That Works as One.*

Applying RMT:
12-Step Workshop Design Process

There are two ways to apply RMT's 5 Elements within your team. You can facilitate the process yourself, or you can engage a team-building facilitator.

No matter which path you choose, you will increase the likelihood of a successful team-building event by using RMT's 12 Steps. If you decide to hire a facilitator, ask them to follow RMT's 12 Steps.

Let's briefly look at the Implementation Plan and the 12-step design process now.

Right-Minded Teamwork Implementation Plan

What is the best way to apply RMT in your team? There is no one answer to this question. However, the three-workshop plan presented here has proven effective countless times. As a key part of RMT's 5 Elements model, you'll notice Work Agreements are incorporated right from the start.

First Workshop – Work Agreements
- Identify team psychological goals and values (Element #2)
- Create at least one team Work Agreement (Element #3)

Second Workshop – Operating System
- Reset and reaffirm business goals (Element #1) and agree on the Team Operating System (Element #4)

Third Workshop - Teammates
- Conduct a Right-Minded Teammate development workshop (Element #5).

90-Day Operating Plan - Ongoing
- Every 90 days, conduct another *Team Performance Factor Assessment,* and then the team meets to assess progress, identify opportunities, take action, and achieve new teamwork improvements.

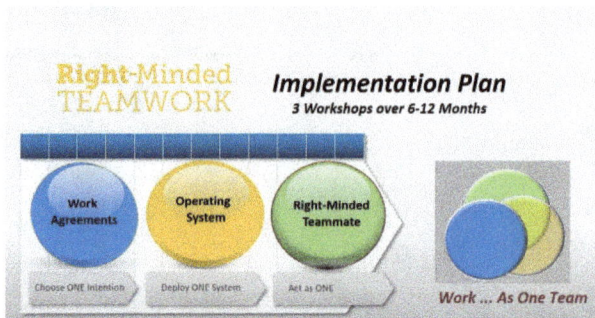

Right-Minded TEAMWORK — Implementation Plan — 3 Workshops over 6-12 Months

Work Agreements — Operating System — Right-Minded Teammate

Choose ONE Intention — Deploy ONE System — Act as ONE

Work ... As One Team

How to Design a Right-Minded, Team-Building Workshop

Ready to design your own transformational Work Agreements workshop? RMT's proven, repeatable 12-step workshop process is organized in three phases:

Contract: Designing the workshop - Steps 1-9

Commence: Facilitating the workshop - Step 10

Carry On: Continuing after the workshop - Steps 11-12

How to Design a
Right-Minded
TEAMWORK
Team-Building Workshop:
12-Step Process

RMT's 12 Steps to effective workshop creation:

Step 1 – Start with the end in mind: Identify the leader's purpose

Step 2 – Leader shares the purpose and outcomes with the facilitator

Step 3 – The leader's desires may be different than the team's needs

Step 4 – Facilitator presents leader with 1st draft team-building plan

Step 5 – Leader announces workshop and prepares teammates

Step 6 – Facilitator conducts Right-Minded Teammate Survey

Step 7 – The facilitator interviews all teammates

Step 8 – Facilitator presents leader with 2nd draft team-building plan

Step 9 – Leader & facilitator finalize and distribute workshop agenda

Step 10 – Facilitator and leader conduct the team-building workshop

Step 11 – The team implements Improvement Plan and tracks results

Step 12 – Leader and facilitator begin designing next team workshop

 To Learn More…

For a complete explanation of RMT's three-workshop Implementation Plan including real-world examples, head over to RightMindedTeamwork.com or your favorite book retailer, and pick up your copy of **Right-Minded Teamwork in Any Team**: *The Ultimate Team Building Method to Create a Team That Works as One.*

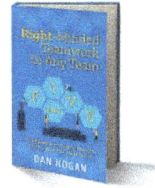

For full details on RMT's 12 Steps workshop design process, go to RightMindedTeamwork.com and search for **Design a Right-Minded, Team-Building Workshop**: *12 Steps to Create a Team That Works as One.*

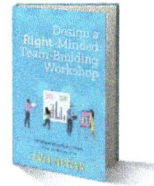

Work Agreements
Require Right Attitudes

Creating and living team Work Agreements is necessary for establishing Right-Minded Teamwork.

To create Work Agreements, your team must first identify the "right" attitudes for the team. Those attitudes form your team's collective, consciously chosen **thought system**. They describe how you will do no harm as you work as one.

Your team's initial set of Right-Minded attitudes is agreed upon during your first team-building workshop, during which you also create your first Work Agreement. After that, they may be adjusted and updated on an as-needed basis.

Meet Your Decision-Maker

The Right-Minded Choice Model teaches that you are the **Decision-Maker.** In every difficult situation, there are two ways you can choose to respond.

At all times, you are mindful, or you are mindless. You are either following your Right Mind, Reason, or your wrong mind, Ego.

When a challenging situation happens, you either:
- accept Ego's guidance and act like a victim or victimizer, or
- embrace Reason and act in an accountable, Right-Minded way, as described in your team Work Agreements.

Even though there are many variations of those two choices, *there are still just two.*

Successful Work Agreements describe how teammates make the Right Choice.

EGO   **DECISION MAKER**   **REASON**

For the background story behind the **RMT Choice Model**, read the RMT book *Reason, Ego, and the Right-Minded Teamwork Myth*. This short story introduces the three characters who live in every teammate's life: Reason, Ego, and the Decision-Maker.

Two Ways to Choose Right-Minded Attitudes for Your Team

Your team's list of "right" attitudes can be short. After you create these values and norms, you will commit to actively living them. Your attitudes and commitment to living them are transformed into your team's written Work Agreements.

Here is an example.

We choose these Right-Minded attitudes as our psychological goals:
- *We accept 100% accountability and responsibility for our thoughts and behaviors.*
- *When we make mistakes, we never punish. We learn. We recover. We do no harm. We work as one.*
- *We positively acknowledge and reward each other.*
- *We are we-centered, never self-centered.*
- *When difficult team situations happen, we accept, forgive, and adjust our attitudes and behavior. We always find solutions because we believe that none of us is as smart as all of us.*
- *When new teammates join our team, we will share these goals and ask them to choose them, too.*

There are two ways you can identify the "right" attitudes and psychological goals for your team.

1. Share the Right-Minded Teammate Attitudes & Behaviors list with the team (see below). Allow teammates to choose a few from that list. Or use those ideas to create goals that fit your team better.

2. Share the Right Choice Model (as described in the RMT book *How to Apply the Right Choice Model: Create a Right-Minded Team That Works as One*).

    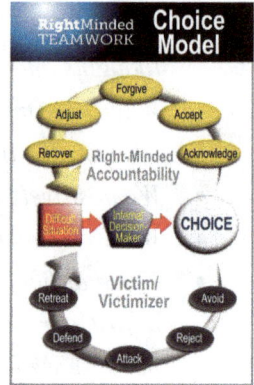

    In a team event, collectively agree on a list of accountable attitudes and work behaviors your team believes will help address your teamwork issues and sustain RMT.

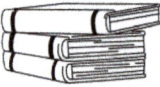

To Learn More…

To learn more about presenting and teaching the Right Choice Model, go to RightMindedTeamwork.com or your favorite book retailer, and pick up your copy of *How to Apply the Right Choice Model: Create a Right-Minded Team That Works as One*.

Making the Right Choice

The Right-Minded Choice Model says you are your own internal Decision-Maker.

This "you" refers to your observer, interpreter, and decider. It is the part of you that sees all your experiences and determines how you will respond to those situations.

Look closely at the Right Choice Model below now.

Do you see yourself, the Decision-Maker, sitting right in the middle between your difficult situation and the choice you must make?

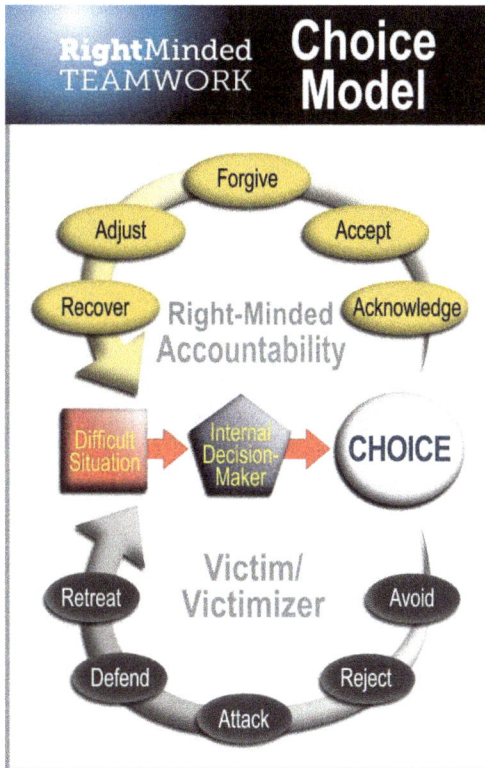

In this position, you are faced with your two options. You can either choose the right direction, the upper loop, by following your Work Agreements – or the wrong direction, the lower loop.

As the Decision-Maker, you are never alone during these moments of choice.

Reason and Ego are always there in your mind, every time you make choices, whether you are conscious of them or not. Each time you make a decision, you either mindfully and consciously choose to follow Reason and your team's Work Agreements, or you mindlessly and unconsciously decide to follow Ego's lessons and wrong-minded thinking.

Choosing the upper loop means **accepting**, **forgiving**, and **adjusting**, which is your mindful move into the Unified Circle of Right-Minded Thinking. In contrast, the lower loop of rejection, Ego attack, and defensiveness describes the divided circle of wrong-minded thinking.

Right-Minded Teamwork encourages teammates to follow Reason and their Work Agreements into the upper circle.

For more about Right-Minded attitudes, look for the section of this book titled "Right-Minded Teamwork Attitudes & Behaviors."

Trust Your Intuition as the Decision-Maker

If thinking about Reason and Ego is new to you, it can be helpful to think of Reason as your positive intuition and Ego as your negative, arrogant, and sometimes even vindictive intuition.

At different times throughout our lives, we all listen to and follow each of these teachers.

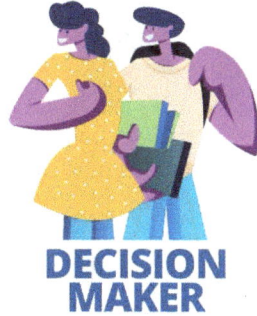

DECISION MAKER

Stop and remember when you had a hunch or feeling about what you should do or say in a particular situation. Did you ignore your intuition? Let's say you did not follow your instinct, and it turned out to be a mistake. What did you say to yourself and others?

I wish I had trusted my intuition!

As this memory illustrates, **you already know how to listen and be mindful** of your intuition. It is your natural pre-separation state of mind. You just need to do it regularly.

If not…

Remember a time when you became angry, agitated, or annoyed with a teammate. Without thinking, you said mean-spirited things. You, too, were saying to yourself, *"My life can't get better until you change."* Accept it. Your negative behavior happened because you did not stop for a **moment of Reason.**

You were literally **out of your Right Mind** as you unconsciously turned towards Ego for guidance.

EGO　　　**DECISION MAKER**　　　**REASON**

During your reaction, you were mindless as you followed Ego's advice. Then, after a while, once you stepped back and calmed down, you could see your behavior was a mistake - only a mistake, to be corrected, not punished. At this moment, you shifted your perspective. You forgave yourself, and you adjusted by apologizing and promising not to behave that way again. You returned to your Right Mind.

If you are not accustomed to trusting your intuition but would like to do so more, you will need to practice.

> *The key is to **pause**, be **still**, and intentionally **listen** for your positive intuition - that **moment of Reason** - before you react to a situation or event.*

It is that simple. But that does not make it easy, especially at first. It takes mindful practice to *train your mind* to listen for this joyous, intuitive moment. It takes an unwavering commitment to stop yourself continually, gently, and compassionately when you become angry, fearful, agitated, or anxious.

It is not always easy, but it can be done. Many have learned this skill. You can, too. As the Decision-Maker, you always have free will regarding whether you choose to follow Ego or Reason. Even if you've tried before and failed, you can start again today.

Remember that even with steadfast commitment, it will take practice to excel. You will make mistakes. That's okay. Return to your Work Agreements. Choose Reason again. And again, and again. When you realize you've chosen Ego, apologize, forgive, correct, and move on. The more you practice, the easier it will get.

You will soon find that as you change your mind, you automatically change your behavior. And when you change your behavior, you transform your team into a lovely learning classroom. The more you make an effort to *be* **in your Right Mind**, the easier it will become to *stay* **in your Right Mind**.

Now, instead of saying, *"I wish I had listened to my intuition,"* you will say,

I'm so glad I turned towards Reason and followed my intuition!

Mindfulness Is Choice in Action

When you are mindless, you don't think or reflect. Instead of *consciously* choosing how to respond, you react *unconsciously* in an emotionally immature way, blaming others or avoiding the situation altogether.

When you're mindful, you reflect and carefully choose how you respond to everything that happens to you and around you. When a problematic situation happens, being mindful means asking yourself this question, which is a core part of the RMT model:

What did I do or say to **create**, **promote**, *or* **allow** *this to happen?*

Your answers to this question help you and your team experience a **moment of Reason**, which paves the way for you to create real solutions.

As an example, let's assume a significant mistake has happened in your team.

Half the team is aggressively blaming the other half for the mistake in what is often called an **"Ego attack."**

RIGHT-MINDED
Accountability

is the **desire, willingness,** and **ability** to change my mind & behavior in order to effectively respond to difficult situations.

This means owning my part in the situation by asking:

"How did I CREATE, PROMOTE, or ALLOW this difficult situation to happen?"

RightMindedTeamwork.com

Teammates are making toxic and hurtful statements, directly and indirectly, about each other. The team is stuck in a battleground of "attack and defend." No one is working to resolve the mistake.

Seeking a **moment of Reason**, you ask yourself,

What am I doing to create, promote, or allow this blaming conversation to continue?

You realize you've been standing by and saying nothing. You were **avoiding**, which is the **first step in the lower loop** of the Right Choice Model.

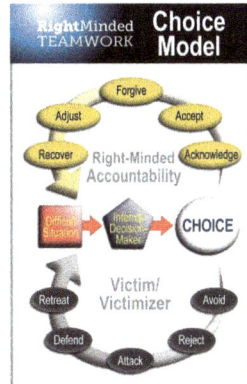

Now that you are aware of your attitude and behavior, you change your mind. You choose to follow Reason and act in a Right-Minded, accountable way, just as your **Work Agreement** states.

Reason is that part of your mind that always speaks for the Right Choice Attitudes & Behaviors. When you are facing a difficult team situation and need a **moment of Reason**, to find the best way to respond to a difficult team situation, say to yourself:

I am here to be truly helpful.

I am here to represent Reason who sent me.

I do not have to worry about what to say or what to do because Reason who sent me will direct me.

As you pause, you are able to remember two Right-Minded responses, both of which are likely part of your Work Agreements:
- Engage in helpful problem-solving communication.
- Correct mistakes rather than punish and blame.

As you reflect, while holding these two choices in your mind and heart, *intuitive* answers come to your *"right"* mind. Now that you have received Reason's advice, in a calm, "do-no-harm-work-as-one" voice, you say,

> *Here's a suggestion. Let's discuss what we know, the facts, about what happened. Then let's find an immediate solution.*
>
> *After we resolve the mistake, let's have a second team discussion, not to blame, but to create a Work Agreement so that this mistake doesn't happen again. How does that sound?*

If you had followed Ego's advice and continued your **avoidance behavior**, the conflict would have continued.

Since you chose to look towards Reason, you created an environment where you and your teammates **recovered** from the mistake, the **final step in the upper loop** of the model.

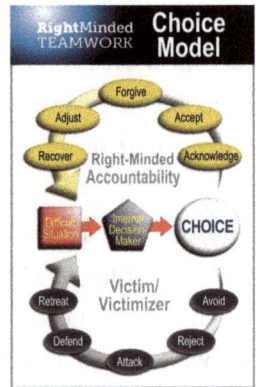

Reason, as always, has brought you - and hopefully everyone else, too - **back into your Right Mind.**

By listening to Reason, trusting your intuition, and following your Work Agreements, you **train your mind** to consistently return to the Unified Circle of Right-Minded Thinking, creating a team environment where you do no harm and work as one.

What Does It Mean to "Train Your Mind?"

When your mind is well-trained, and a difficult team situation happens, you immediately stop for a moment of Reason. You remember your Work Agreements, and you consciously choose to follow them.

> *Training your mind simply means practicing your team's* **Work Agreements***, and your psychological goals, especially during difficult team situations.*

By actively asking the question, "How did I **create**, **promote**, or **allow** this difficult situation to happen?" and then **stepping back in your mind** to listen for the answers, you will learn to hear and implicitly trust Reason's voice. Over time, this practice s*hifts your perception* to finding solutions, allowing you to *hear the best answers* to the questions you ask.

Once you know how to tune in to Reason to receive those answers, you will always know how to behave and respond.

So, how do you know when you are really hearing the voice of Reason and not Ego?

Firstly, answers from Reason will bring you a feeling of *inner peace* and *confidence*.

Secondly, you will know you've heard Reason when *the answer you have received heals and resolves the difficulty* you face *while doing no harm* to anyone.

If your solution meets both of these criteria, rest assured you are listening to Reason.

Over time, as you train your mind, it will become easier and easier for you to forgive the errors and mistakes of yourself and your teammates. You will simply recognize them, accept them, and immediately move toward finding solutions.

The Constantly Complaining Teammate (CCT)

Here's an example of how to **successfully train your mind**.

Think about a team experience where you've had to deal with a "CCT" - a Constantly Complaining Teammate.

In your mind, what do you picture when you see and interact with this person?

If what you see in your mind's eye is a big angry dog, ready to attack you and others, you are seeing the CCT through your Ego's eyes. You believe they are to be feared and avoided.

It is the perspective of an untrained and unforgiving mind. But it doesn't have to stay that way.

Alternatively, you can choose to follow Reason. When you genuinely desire to follow Reason's guidance, and you practice being mindful of your thoughts and choices, your perspective changes.

With Reason's help, instead of seeing your CCT as a vicious dog ready to attack, your new perception now shows you a cute-though-angry puppy. It is now *impossible* to fear them, and there is certainly no valid reason to avoid them.

With your new and healed perspective, you reinterpret the CCT's complaints as mistakes that need correction, not punishment. You accept their complaints as *their call for help,* not an attack.

Instead of reacting negatively, you say to yourself:

I will do my best to forgive this person for their constantly complaining behavior because I honestly think they care about doing a good job, even if they communicate poorly.

I will listen to their complaints. I'll ask clarifying questions to be sure I fully understand.

I will be kind, compassionate, non-judgmental, and civil in the way I respond. I will not get defensive. I will do no harm. I'll ask how we should resolve the situation.

When this Right-Minded perception shift happens, you will finally see your CCT for who they really are.

> *Rather than a person to be feared, avoided, harmed, or dismissed, your teammate is now a worthy sister or brother who wants to be heard, included, and helped – by YOU.*

They truly deserve no less than your Right-Minded, caring, and loving response.

Return to the Unified Circle of Right-Minded Thinking

When your team discusses and agrees on your psychological goals – your consciously chosen set of attitudes and behaviors as described in your Work Agreements – you have created your team's collective thought system.

By uniting with each other in this way and openly committing to one another through your Work Agreements, you are renouncing Ego in yourself and your teammates and collectively committing to train your minds to follow Reason.

This process of creating team Work Agreements is your undivided declaration of interdependence. Your assertion is saying,

> *We hold these mindful truths to be self-evident that all minds are created equal, and whosoever believes that will have everlasting freedom to choose Right-Minded teamwork.*

Your declaration plus your daily acts of living your team Work Agreements *is your return* to the forgiving Unified Circle Right-Minded Thinking.

The one fundamental freedom no one can take away from you is your **freedom to choose** how to respond to life's challenges.

At every moment, your Decision-Maker is making that choice in one of two ways: Either your Decision-Maker is choosing based on Ego's wrong-minded dictates or Reason's Right-Minded principles and your team's Work Agreements.

Follow Reason, and you declare your freedom from Ego's battlefields.

Follow Reason, and you have joined others who hold these Right-Minded thoughts to be self-evident and true.

Follow Reason, and you transform your fixed perspectives by reinterpreting attack behaviors as a call for help – your help.

*Follow Reason, and your team will agree on a Right-Minded set of attitudes and behaviors as described in your **Work Agreements**.*

*By following **Reason** and your **Work Agreements**, you will renounce Ego while uniting with your fellow teammates.*

You will return to your ultimate goal, the forgiving Unified Circle of Right-Minded Thinking.

Right-Minded Teamwork Attitudes & Behaviors

Over decades of team-building work, I worked with hundreds of teams. Along the way, I collected their Right-Minded attitudes and behaviors into a list of choices that I grouped into **work behaviors** and **work processes**.

Use these lists to form your team's Psychological Goals and Work Agreements, either by adopting them or adapting them.

Was I Born with These Thoughts & Attitudes?

Thoughts and attitudes always precede teamwork behavior.

Right-Minded attitudes come from Reason. Wrong-minded attitudes come from Ego.

The good news is that Right-Minded attitudes are natural. They are already inside you and your teammates.

When you think about any of the wrong-minded Ego attitudes listed below, ask yourself,

Was I born with these depressing, debilitating, and awful attitudes?

Your answer will always be **"no!"** You learned those wrong-minded attitudes from Ego. That means *you can unlearn them, too.*

You *Can* Change Your Mind

In 35 years of team-building facilitation, I heard too many well-intentioned albeit wrong-minded teammates say,

> *That's just the way I am. I can't change.*

That is ***simply not true***.

What is true is that they refused to change their minds.

> *When someone says they cannot change, what they are really saying is their behavior is more powerful than their mind.*

When they realize and joyfully accept that ***their mind is in charge***, they open the way for happiness, inner peace, and Right-Minded Teamwork.

Why You Want to Change Your Perspective

Fixed perspectives prevent you from achieving Right-Minded Teamwork. Your limiting beliefs, interpretations, and lessons from Ego are blocks to Right-Minded Thinking.

To remove those blocks, you must transform your self-limiting thoughts. The first of RMT's 7 Mindfulness Training Lessons will help you do that.

Lesson one of the 7 Mindfulness Training Lessons states, *"I am never upset for the reason I think."*

Reminding yourself of this truth when you or your teammates are out of your Right mind will help you experience a **moment of Reason**. Instead of seeing your teammate's behavior as a negative Ego attack, you are able to reinterpret their behavior as a desperate **call for help** from you and your teammates.

With this new insight, you are able to respond to your teammate with Reason's wise guidance. With Reason's help, you have effectively changed your perspective.

. . . . .

The 30 Right-Minded Teamwork Attitudes & Behaviors starting on the next page will help you change your perspective and achieve Right-Minded Thinking.

Work Behavior Attitudes

As the Decision-Maker, You Behave One Way or the Other!

EGO   **DECISION MAKER**   **REASON**

Demonstrate adversarial competition and power struggles	Demonstrate collaborative competition and synergy
Demonstrate victim or victimizer attitudes & behaviors	Exhibit accountable and responsible attitudes & behavior
Worry that "I am my mistakes;" continue to obsess over mistakes	Embrace that "I am not my mistakes;" mistakes are opportunities for me to learn
Noticeable lack of emotional maturity and empathy	Desire to be emotionally mature and compassionate
Exhibit self-centered attitudes	Exhibit we-centered attitudes
Hold & project grievances; Never forget or forgive	Embrace & extend forgiveness; Let go of issues from the past
After mistakes, helplessness occurs, and I choose to give up or not try as hard	After mistakes, forgiveness occurs, and I choose to try again and again

Work Behavior Attitudes (Continued)

There's a mindset of scarcity, a belief that to give is to lose	There's an attitude of abundance, a belief that to give is to receive
There is suspicion, closed-mindedness, and resistance to change	There is readiness and open-mindedness for positive change
Too often, people restate their position, believing they are right, and others are wrong	We always seek mutual understanding: believing together, we are right
I believe I'm the smartest, and I can prove it	We believe none of us is as smart as all of us
I demonstrate a conscious or unconscious attitude of confusion, chaos, complexity, and drama	We continually demonstrate a conscious attitude of clarity, order, simplicity, and calmness
There's a widespread belief that difficult team situations and changes determine how we feel	We know for sure that our minds determine how we feel about difficult situations or changes
We believe it is best to keep quiet when correction is needed	We have a team culture of appropriately speaking up when a correction is needed
We believe in these attitudes: vulnerability, unkindness, hate, attack, blame	We embrace these attitudes: invulnerability, love, kindness, do no harm, work as one

Work Behavior Attitudes (Continued)

We believe in power over others	We believe in power with others
Growth is painful; remember, if there is no pain, there is no gain	Growth doesn't have to be painful; learning is joyously attained and gladly remembered
It is best to do unto others (reject, attack, defend) before they do unto you	We do unto others (accept, forgive, adjust) as we would have them do unto us
There is a feeling of avoidance and criticism among teammates	There is a spirit of acknowledgment and reward among teammates
There is a love and a need for power, fame, money, and pleasure	We strive for non-attachment to power, fame, money, and pleasure
Our team is a battleground where conflict is prolonged as we act like victims or victimizers	Our team is our learning classroom where conflict is resolved as we act like Right-Minded Teammates
There is mistrust, fear, and lack of safety among teammates	There is trust, peace, and safety among teammates
Defensiveness is prevalent in our team	Defenselessness is widespread in our team

Process Behavior Attitudes

Your Team Can Operate One Way or the Other!

The team's purpose, vision, and mission are unclear and not supported	Our team continuously clarifies our purpose, vision, and mission and actively supports them
There is no discernable team operating system	There is an efficient, continuous improvement team operating system in place
There is a predominant attitude of avoidance and complaining	We have an attitude and a system for acknowledgment and reward
Disagreements and a lack of clear roles and responsibilities exist	We periodically clarify teammate roles and responsibilities
We are unclear who makes decisions and how	Our team has a clear and effective decision-making Work Agreement
We spend too much time and energy applying inefficient work processes	Our work processes and procedures are clear, understood, accepted, and efficient
Too often, people are punished for making mistakes	We always embrace an attitude of converting mistakes into learning opportunities

Actionable Attitudes = Better Behaviors

The Right-Minded attitudes in these charts are practical. However, these noble thoughts and attitudes will do no good unless you discuss them and define what they mean for your team.

Once you have identified and defined the behaviors associated with your chosen attitudes, captured in your team Work Agreements, you must also make the conscious choice to live them going forward.

Don't let your team's insignificant, Ego-driven squabbles pull you down. Be vigilant and demonstrate by your actions and behaviors that you have risen above your old, petty, teamwork battleground issues.

Be vigilant and demonstrate by your actions and behaviors that you have risen above your old, petty, teamwork battleground issues.

No team situation can pull you into Ego's realm of conflict when you believe it is far better to collaborate and win than argue and lose.

Remember, it is from your collective Right Mind that you create your Work Agreements. And when you make and follow your promises, you are uniting with each other without the Ego. When you do that, you have returned to the United Circle of Right-Minded Thinking. From that unified circle, it will be much easier to recover from any difficult team situation because you have, at that moment, restored your team's collective Right Mind to Reason.

The 10 Characteristics of Right-Minded Teammates

Right-Minded Teammates have diverse backgrounds, vastly different experiences, and display a wide range of skills. No two are alike. Still, there are certain characteristics all Right-Minded Teammates share.

These characteristics align the teammate's authentic self with the RMT motto of *Do no harm, and work as one*. They are:

1. Trust
2. Honesty
3. Tolerance
4. Gentleness
5. Joy
6. Defenselessness
7. Generosity
8. Patience
9. Open-mindedness
10. Faithfulness

When you help your team create and live team Work Agreements, they will be well on their way to living these characteristics.

How does the Right-Minded Teammate live these characteristics?

They do two things when difficult situations occur.

First, they remind themselves of their commitment to *thinking* in a do-no-harm way. Second, they choose to demonstrate do-no-harm *behaviors* that align with their Right-Minded attitudes, such as finding solutions to challenging situations.

It is not always easy to do these two things, but it is always that simple.

To encourage your team to embrace and live these Right-Minded characteristics, check out these two RMT books:

*7 **Mindfulness Training Lessons:*** *Improve Teammates' Ability to Work as One with Right-Minded Thinking* will teach you how to apply RMT's seven, powerful thinking lessons to encourage Right-Minded, unified teamwork.

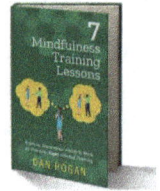

How to Apply the Right Choice Model: *Create a Right-Minded Team That Works as One* teaches you how to transform a disappointed team customer into a 100% satisfied customer by making Right-Minded choices, all of which align with the above list of characteristics.

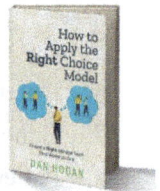

For now, though, let's take a closer look at each of these 10, Right-Minded Teammate characteristics.

1. Trust

Trust is the foundational characteristic for teammates who desire to create and sustain Right-Minded Teamwork. Right-Minded Teammates trust one another because their own past experience has taught them that, in all situations, a forgiving attitude creates safety for teammates to collaborate and resolve difficulties.

2. Honesty

For the Right-Minded Teammate, honesty means more than just telling the truth. It refers to consistency in thought and deed. An honest, Right-Minded Teammate is consistently looking within and striving to align thoughts, words, and behaviors with the team's psychological goals and forgiving values. This kind of honesty is essential to creating and sustaining Right-Minded Teamwork.

3. Tolerance

Judgment is the opposite of forgiveness; it implies a lack of trust. Tolerance indicates non-judgment. Tolerant teammates do not judge one another because they know that though they are not the same, all Right-Minded Teammates are equal. Their tolerance creates space for the wisdom of diversity to surface, and their equality allows them to work together as one.

4. Gentleness

Right-Minded Teammates believe that gentleness is the only sane response to challenging situations and circumstances. Whereas harshness and judgment close doors, gentleness opens them. With gentleness, it is easy for teammates to do no harm as they work as one – with teammates and customers alike.

5. Joy

Joy is the inevitable result of Right-Minded teammates who are gentle and non-judgmental. Fear is impossible for those who are gentle, especially during challenging situations. Joy comes from gentleness, tolerance, honesty, and forgiveness.

6. Defenselessness

Right-Minded Teammates understand that defenses are foolish, judgmental attitudes and behaviors that prevent the team from finding solutions to difficult situations. When teammates summon the courage to forgive and trust themselves and to look honestly at their wrong-minded defenses without judgment, they can lay those debilitating arguments gently aside, creating the proper conditions for honestly doing no harm and working as one.

7. Generosity

Right-Minded Teammates honestly and humbly give all they know to help their team create Right-Minded Teamwork and achieve 100% customer satisfaction. The world teaches that if you give something away, you lose it, but Right-Minded Teammates realize that to give *is* to receive. They eagerly participate with their teammates to create solutions to solve challenging situations, bringing joy and satisfaction to the team through their gentle generosity.

8. Patience

Teammates who know Right-Minded Teamwork is the outcome they want can easily afford to wait without concern. Because their goal is to be tolerant and gentle with their teammates, patience comes naturally. The highest desire is to work as one.

9. Open-Mindedness

Judgment, or wrong-mindedness, closes teammates' minds, creating resistance to Right-Minded Teamwork. To ensure they do no harm while working as one, Right-Minded Teammates embrace open-mindedness, also known as Right-Mindedness.

10. Faithfulness

Faithfulness describes a teammate's trust in their team's version of Right-Minded Teamwork. When a teammate is faithful, they effortlessly and wholeheartedly believe in Right-Minded Teamwork. They *want* to do no harm and work as one. They know none of us is as smart as all of us. When applied during challenging circumstances, their faithfulness inevitably leads the team to happy outcomes.

Real-World Applications for Right Choice & Work Agreements

The **Right Choice Model** and team **Work Agreements** are perfect for those situations where logic and other fact-based processes don't work. Here are several instances where these tools lend themselves well.

Team Building – When a team is "storming," the Choice Model and Work Agreements will help you facilitate a positive recovery in team members' attitudes and behaviors.

Benefit: The team focuses its energy on accomplishing real team business instead of complaining about other team members.

Leadership Development – Successful leaders guide their direct reports to higher and higher levels of accountability, which is an inherent result of Right Choice and Work Agreements.

Benefit: The team addresses problems head-on versus whining and complaining about difficult work situations.

Safety – This Choice Model is a perfect companion for behavioral safety strategies and training programs because "choice" is the precursor to "safe" behavior.

Benefit: Adds the final layer of understanding in safety training by establishing a "thinking system" clearly defined in the team's Work Agreements.

Diversity – A lack of willingness to embrace diversity indicates wrong-minded, victim/victimizer choices. Introducing the Right Choice Model raises awareness of these choices in a gentle way and creating Work Agreements clearly establishes a culture of equality.

Benefit: Surfacing existing disconnects between teammates and addressing them in a forgiving way allows for higher levels of collaboration.

Alliance Partnerships – Too often, partnerships break up or fail to meet expectations because of the business' attitudes and behaviors. Using the Right Choice Model allows partnership issues to be addressed in an emotionally mature way, and Work Agreements can capture agreed-upon ways of collaborating moving forward.

Benefit: By redirecting dysfunctional behaviors, new energy can be put towards accomplishing the alliance's work.

Change Management – Consultants and leaders can use the Choice Model and Work Agreements to accomplish new change initiatives.

Benefit: This Choice Model and team Work Agreements increase the likelihood of achieving success by gently removing restraining forces.

Individual Effectiveness – We all feel and act like victims from time to time; the key is not getting stuck in "victim headspace." To avoid getting stuck, we must identify those situations that drive us into wrong-mindedness.

Benefit: The Right Choice Model, when used as a personal assessment, helps you identify personal emotional triggers, which is the first step in effective change management.

Outsourcing – When outsourcing must happen, the Choice Model and Work Agreements will help ensure a smooth transition.

Benefit: By identifying those who are more apt to accept and embrace change (versus those who believe they deserve special treatment) and clearly communicating the choices and attitudes that are expected, outsourcing is more likely to succeed.

Other – The possibilities for the Right Choice Model and Work Agreement process are genuinely endless. In any conflict situation, these tools will assist in facilitating positive transformation.

The Work Agreement Facilitation Process

Now that all teammates have chosen their Right Attitudes and embraced the Right Choice Model philosophy, you are ready to create your Work Agreements.

Nearly all teamwork issues can be addressed and resolved with Work Agreements.

Two Types of Work Agreements

A **process Work Agreement** describes who will do what and the work methods they will use. It defines work tasks in terms of roles, responsibilities, interfaces, or procedures.

One essential process Agreement is a team's Decision-Making Work Agreement. RMT advocates every team create such an Agreement as early as possible. Without one, the team will likely encounter many unnecessary interpersonal dysfunctions and work mistakes. We'll talk more about Decision-Making Agreements in a moment.

A **behavioral Work Agreement** describes how people will behave while they perform their tasks, such as the ways teammates will bring to light, communicate, and resolve difficult performance issues or interpersonal conflicts. This type of Work Agreement aims for transparency in all such interactions.

A Work Agreement that is wholeheartedly agreed upon includes an **Intention** statement that defines your team's choice as well as **Clarifications or Conditions** for acceptance. Here is an example.

. . . . .

Intention:

1. Each teammate will communicate their thoughts and feelings in appropriate ways.

Clarifications or Conditions:

A. We follow the spirit and intent of our company values.
B. If we believe another person is communicating inappropriately, we will call it to their attention in private.
C. Even though this Agreement addresses inappropriate communication behaviors, we also agree to give positive teammate reinforcement when we see and hear excellent communication.

Below you will find two real examples of Work Agreements. The first one is a **behavioral** team communication Work Agreement. The other is a **process** Work Agreement around decision-making.

I worked with this team for a few years. These were phenomenally successful Work Agreements because teammates passionately created and actively lived them day in and day out.

The communication Work Agreement directly below is also used as a teaching device in this book. In the pages to come, I will show you how that team created this Agreement.

Real Team Work Agreements

Behavioral Agreement – Communication

Team Choice: Intention Statement
1. Each teammate will communicate in a respectful way.

Clarifications / Conditions for Acceptance:

A. We will use good communication techniques that include appropriate body language and tone of voice, plus suitable words.
B. If we see or hear disrespect or we hear an inappropriate behind-the-back conversation, we own it and need to step in.
C. If someone unintentionally shows disrespect, we will give them the benefit of the doubt, let them know, and create a new way to interact going forward.
D. We will actively support team decisions in word, deed, and energy; we will use our decision-making protocol agreement for key decisions.
E. We will be on time for meetings.
F. We will ask, "May I interrupt you?"
G. We will use observable facts during disagreements and decision-making, and we will acknowledge when we are using assumptions.
H. We will understand each other's roles, ask for help if we need it, share relevant information and if helpful, give constructive feedback in private.
I. If someone continues to break this agreement, we will tell them that we will invite a third party to help if there is continued disagreement. If that doesn't solve the issues, we will all go to a higher authority for support and resolution.

Process Agreement – Decision-Making Protocol

Team Choice: Intention Statement
2. We will go for consensus for all key team decisions, but our fallback will be that Maria [team leader] will decide if we cannot reach a consensus.

Conditions for Acceptance / Clarification
A. Before entering a discussion, we'll agree on the decision-making method and fall back, plus when [date] a decision will be made.
B. Before delving into a solution, we will create an opportunity or problem statement.
C. At the beginning of our discussion, we will determine boundaries & givens (i.e., time sensitivity; cost, hassle, impact, 80% or 100% perfect decision, etc.).
D. We provide a business case (appropriate justification) for our decision, including cost/benefit.
E. During our conversations, we will advocate and inquire. We will not hold back. For instance, we will acknowledge assumptions and facts.
F. To create the best solutions, we will also think about alternative ways to test our solution (Devil's Advocate).
G. If we find ourselves at an impasse, we will call a "time out" to calm down or acquire more technical information.
H. When a decision is made, we will accurately represent and support the decision.
I. We do this agreement because we want to improve teamwork and trust in one another.
J. We will hold ourselves and others accountable for living the letter and the spirit of this agreement; we will fine-tune it as necessary

Facilitating Work Agreements: Don't Do This!

A Reason-able idea…
Don't present another team's Agreements to go by.

As an aspiring Work Agreements facilitator, it is advantageous to review and learn from other teams' Work Agreements, especially to understand what worked and didn't work.

However, I cannot overemphasize the importance of *not* making it a standard practice to present another team's Work Agreements as "go-by" examples during facilitation.

Each team needs to invest *its own efforts* into *its own Work Agreements.*

Teammates who put genuine effort into discussing and agreeing on how they will resolve their particular team challenges increase the likelihood of actually *living* their Work Agreements going forward.

Why? Because they worked hard to create their Work Agreement. They agreed that living them is in their best, shared interest. They know their unique Work Agreements have not been imposed on them arbitrarily.

There's also one more thing you should not do: Don't announce or explain the 10 Steps outlined in this book to teammates. These 10 Steps are designed to help you plan, organize, and efficiently facilitate the Work Agreement process.

Facilitation: Do This!

When your team creates its first Work Agreement, remember:

1. It always takes longer to facilitate a team's first Work Agreement.
2. As the facilitator, you want to be on the lookout for your chance to help the team create a "moment of Reason" amongst themselves.

Why the First Work Agreement Takes Longer

The first time around, teammates will not be familiar with the Work Agreement process, so everyone will be learning as they go. Teammates also won't have had a chance to experience the effectiveness of Work Agreements for themselves yet, either. After they finalize their first Work Agreement, the team will take much less time discussing and creating future Agreements because they will clearly understand the process and understand the benefits.

As you introduce the concept of Work Agreements for the first time, aim to create only one or two key Work Agreements. Keeping things simple will allow the team to learn the process and still come out of their team workshop with actionable Work Agreements. If more are needed, they can always be created in subsequent workshops.

It's also practical for teammates to think of their Work Agreements as *evergreen*. If they determine their Work Agreements are not quite right or don't accomplish their desired outcome, Agreements can and should be modified. It's worth noting that **process Work Agreements** usually require fewer modifications after the workshop than **behavioral Work Agreements**.

Creating a process Work Agreement is also typically a little easier to facilitate because it deals with relatively impersonal policies, procedures, or methods. Most people are more comfortable discussing these topics than delving into interpersonal issues or explaining how they should behave. Later in this book, when we get to the detailed explanation of the 10 Steps to create team Work Agreements, you will read a true story that illustrates this common reaction.

The process of turning day-to-day activities and decisions into a future-state flow chart with your team is usually not emotional or confrontational. But when a team is faced with difficult human interaction issues such as low trust, poor communication, toxic behavior, personality conflicts, or lack of accountability, and you are creating behavioral Work Agreements, different perspectives can easily be interpreted as judgmental, which often leads to more self-perpetuating dysfunction.

However, both process Work Agreements and behavioral Work Agreements have their place. Process Agreements are used to solve teamwork workflow issues, and behavioral Agreements are best used to identify and describe interpersonal behaviors the team will use to resolve their conflicts.

Looking for Moments of Reason

When you experience a positive and often surprising moment of revelation, clarity, or sanity regarding a particular challenge, you have achieved a moment of Reason. Reason's teaching breaks through, bringing you back from being out of your right mind. These moments occur when teammates genuinely try to recover from an Ego attack.

Moments of Reason are a magnificent cornerstone of Right-Minded Thinking. As you begin to train your mind, they may be slow to occur, but with practice, moments of Reason will come more easily. When they do, you feel confident and at peace. You know what you need to do, what to say, and to whom. You rise above the battleground, enter Reason's classroom, and return to the forgiving Unified Circle of Right-Minded Thinking. You do no harm and work as one.

These are the kinds of transformative moments you can help bring about for your team as an RMT facilitator. Especially when you facilitate your team's first Work Agreement, you want to look for and help the team create a moment of Reason. The collective commitment following their moment of Reason will lead them to make the right Work Agreements to solve their current challenges. It happens every time, and it will happen for you. I promise.

A team may experience a moment of Reason either because of something a teammate has said aloud during the workshop or because of something you have said as their facilitator. Either way, as soon as it happens, positively acknowledge the team's mental shift away from Ego and back into their collective Right Mind.

How do you know you have witnessed a moment of Reason? You'll hear a statement like, *"We've already agreed on how we were to address that issue, haven't we?"*

This was the exact phrase I heard in a team's RMT workshop. When the team realized they had created Work Agreements three months prior that addressed the issue they were re-arguing, they immediately shifted back into their collective Right Mind and recommitted to their Work Agreements, effectively ending their conflict.

To Learn More...

You'll read the full story of this team's Work Agreements journey following the detailed description of the 10 Steps.

If you can't wait, skip ahead to the section titled *Sustaining Team Work Agreements,* then look for the question,

"We've already agreed on how to address that issue, haven't we?"

Decision-Making Work Agreements

A team's Decision-Making Work Agreement clearly defines how decisions are made and who makes them. If your team does not already have a Decision-Making Work Agreement, decision-making is an excellent topic to choose as the teamwork topic to address in your first Work Agreements workshop.

RMT advocates every team create such a Decision-Making Work Agreement as early as possible. Without one, the team will likely encounter many unnecessary interpersonal dysfunctions and work mistakes. I'm confident your own experience has already shown you this is true, which is why it makes good business sense to create one and include it in your team's Operating System.

It's also a good idea in team meetings to remind teammates of your Decision-Making Work Agreement. Doing so will prevent many conflicts.

If you do not currently have a Decision-Making Agreement or you have not updated yours lately, make it a priority.

Below you will find a description of several different decision-making approaches. Use these options to help you create an effective Agreement for your team.

Range of Decision-Making Options

There is no one right way to construct your Decision-Making Agreement, but here are some guidelines and definitions that will help.

1. Command

In this option, the leader decides and announces their decision to teammates. This option is suitable for emergency situations and inconsequential types of decisions. Ideally, when the leader announces their choice, teammates will happily abide by the leader's decision.

2. Consult

The leader gathers information and recommendations in small group meetings or with others outside the team. As with the command option, teammates happily abide by the decision when the leader announces their choice.

3. Consensus

In this option, the team desires to reach a consensus. Everyone has equal authority to persuade and advocate for what they believe to be the best decision.

Consensus does not mean that everyone agrees. What it means is that everyone will **actively support** the decision in word and deed even if they did not get everything they wanted. By actively supporting the decision, teammates are **living** their RMT motto of *"none of us is as smart as all of us."*

Before the team discusses an issue, create a fallback decision-making option if the team cannot reach a consensus. For example, you might agree that the majority of votes wins. Or you could default to a Subject Matter Expert or the team leader to make the final decision in the case of no consensus. There is no perfect fallback, but having one before discussing the problem that needs a decision is highly recommended.

4. Delegation

In this option, the leader gives the team or a subgroup the authority to decide *if* they adhere to specific guidelines and boundaries.

When the group announces their choice, the leader and teammates will abide by the group's decision.

Decision-Making Guidelines

Use some or all of these guidelines in your team's Decision-Making Work Agreement.

An effective Decision-Making Work Agreement requires facilitating the team through two different activities. First, *define the problem* and, second, *solve the problem.*

For important decisions, always allow enough time to discuss the issue thoroughly to ensure you properly define the problem.

Frequently remind teammates of your RMT motto: **None of us is as smart as all of us**.

It's best to avoid debates. If you decide to play a devil's advocate role, announce it in advance.

It's also best not to immediately settle for majority rule, compromises, or trade-offs. Always go into every discussion by looking for a win-win solution.

It's best not to interpret a teammate's silence as support. For some decisions, ask each person to state out loud why they support the decision.

Decide what the group will tell others outside the team about the decision. If necessary, script a standard communication that all agree to follow.

Once they make the decision, the team must reach a consensus.

What Is Consensus?

Consensus is not the same as 100% agreement. It does mean that all teammates agree to *actively support the team's decision*, in word and deed, even though it might not be their personal choice.

How do you know you have reached a consensus? Each teammate can say with confidence:

> *My personal views and ideas have been listened to and seriously considered.*
>
> *I have openly listened to and seriously considered the ideas and views of every other team member.*
>
> *Whether or not this decision would have been my choice, I will actively support it and work towards its implementation and success.*

An Actual Decision-Making Work Agreement

In this book, you will find two real-world Work Agreement examples.

The first one is a behavioral Communication Agreement, and the other is the **Decision-Making Work Agreement** below.

I worked with this team for a few years. They were phenomenally successful because teammates passionately created and actively lived their Agreements day in and day out.

Process Agreement – Decision-Making Protocol

Team Choice: Intention Statement

2. We will go for consensus for all key team decisions, but our fallback will be that Maria [team leader] will decide if we cannot reach a consensus.

Conditions for Acceptance / Clarification

A. Before entering a discussion, we'll agree on the decision-making method and fall back, plus when [date] a decision will be made.

B. Before delving into a solution, we will create an opportunity or problem statement.

C. At the beginning of our discussion, we will determine boundaries & givens (i.e., time sensitivity; cost, hassle, impact, 80% or 100% perfect decision, etc.).

D. We provide a business case (appropriate justification) for our decision, including cost/benefit.

E. During our conversations, we will advocate and inquire. We will not hold back. For instance, we will acknowledge assumptions and facts.

F. To create the best solutions, we will also think about alternative ways to test our solution (Devil's Advocate).

G. If we find ourselves at an impasse, we will call a "time out" to calm down or acquire more technical information.

H. When a decision is made, we will accurately represent and support the decision.

I. We do this agreement because we want to improve teamwork and trust in one another.

J. We will hold ourselves and others accountable for living the letter and the spirit of this agreement; we will fine-tune it as necessary

Facilitating Work Agreements –
A Brief Narrative Overview

Below, you will find three versions of the 10 Steps to creating team Work Agreements:

- a short, narrative description of the Steps
- a graphical representation of the process including real-world examples of the flipcharts created during each Step
- a detailed description of each of the 10 Steps.

By the end of this section, you will have a clear understanding of what it takes to facilitate team Work Agreements.

. . . . .

Let's start by assuming a team leader has decided to conduct a one-day RMT Work Agreements workshop and has asked you to facilitate it. Here are your preparation and facilitation steps.

First Decide: In-Person or Virtual Workshop?

An in-person workshop is a superior choice because teammates can see and feel each other's attitudes and behaviors, which supports the creation of solid, all-in Work Agreements. However, if you must conduct a virtual workshop, the principles, concepts, and steps presented here still apply. Use a video software conferencing platform to ensure all participants can see each other and a virtual flipchart for capturing your team Work Agreements.

Preparation Steps 1-3

Take these three steps before the workshop.

1. Agree on the first teamwork topic to address, which will result in a Work Agreement.
2. Determine the topic's desired outcome.
3. Design an opening question to be asked to kick off the topic dialogue.

In **Step 1**, the team leader informs you, the facilitator, what they want to achieve and why. Often, some difficult situation has occurred that has precipitated the desire for this workshop.

After you understand the leader's desired teamwork outcomes, you interview all teammates to understand what they want to achieve and why.

After the teammate interviews, you share the team's collective input with the leader, which results in selecting the teamwork topics to address in the first workshop.

In our teaching example, we will focus on two specific teamwork outcomes for our workshop: improving communication and improving team decision-making. The first is a behavioral issue, and the second is a work process issue.

In **Step 2**, an agenda is created that includes the desired outcomes.

In **Step 3,** an opening question is created for both issues: communication and decision-making. As the facilitator, you will ask these questions to launch a team discussion that, eventually, leads to one or more Work Agreements.

Facilitation Steps 4-10

4. During your workshop, when the time is right, ask the opening question for your topic.
5. Capture legitimate behavioral answers on a flipchart.
6. Write and propose an intention statement.
7. After a short dialogue, ask if teammates agree to live the intention.
8. Write clarifications and conditions for acceptance.
9. Create an interlocking accountability condition.
10. When everyone approves the Work Agreement, celebrate. Then move to the next topic.

The Workshop

Imagine you are 10 minutes into your workshop. The team leader has welcomed everyone. All teammates have agreed to the desired teamwork outcomes as well as the agenda, ground rules, and the day's logistics.

Before you ask your opening question, take five minutes to introduce or review the Right Choice Model. Your goal is to present the Model in such a way that when you finish teaching it, all teammates declare,

Of course, we need to approach [our issue] in a Right-Minded, accountable way. Let's get started.

Alternatively, the team leader may present the Right Choice Model by relating it to a current team challenge.

To learn more about the Right Choice Model and how to apply it in your team, go to RightMindedTeamwork.com or your favorite book retailer, and pick up your copy of ***How to Apply the Right Choice Model**: Create a Right-Minded Team That Works as One.* Within the book, look for the section titled, "How to Present & Apply the Right Choice Model in Your Team." There, you will find specific instructions on how to present the Right Choice Model successfully.

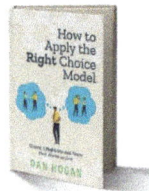

Once the team agrees to take a Right-Minded approach to address their issues, you are ready for your opening question.

Asking the opening question, **Step 4**, should invite an honest discussion on the first teamwork topic. For example, if improving team communication is the desired objective, you might ask, *"If we communicated respectfully, what would you see or hear teammates say or do, or not say or do?"*

Up to this point in the workshop, you, the facilitator, have been doing most of the talking. After asking the opening question, you move into listening, observing, and facilitating.

Now that the opening question has been asked, you listen to the team's discussion, which may last 30 to 60 minutes. All the while, you capture legitimate behavioral answers on a flipchart - **Step 5**.

In **Step 6**, while teammates continue to discuss their workshop topic, you think about and write an intention statement. The proposed statement should evolve from the team's list of behavioral answers. When the time is right, you suggest the intention statement, which, in our example, might sound like, *"Each teammate will communicate in a respectful way with each other and our customers."*

In **Step 7**, you ask teammates if they will agree to live the proposed intention. Most of the time, teammates agree, though they may assert it needs more work. This brings you to Step 8.

In **Step 8,** the team discusses their specific clarifications or conditions for acceptance of the intention statement. As teammates add and edit their conditions, you periodically ask them, *"If you truly lived your Work-Agreement-in-progress, would you achieve your desired outcome?"* Most of the time, they will say yes. This "yes" motivates the team to continue making the "right" Agreement for the team.

Finally, **Step 9** calls for "interlocking accountability" within the Work Agreement - a key part of encouraging the team to live their Agreements day in and day out. Fortunately, you will only need to create interlocking accountability once as it will apply to all Work Agreements.

For a real-world example of interlocking accountability, revisit the "Real Team Work Agreements" several pages back, and look at the final condition in the behavioral communication Agreement.

In **Step 10**, every teammate publicly commits to hold themselves and others accountable for upholding the team Work Agreement. At this point, everyone should genuinely believe the Agreement will help the team achieve its goals.

NOTE: It is not unusual for teammates to break their Work Agreements after the workshop. Often, this breach is just an honest mistake, or a habit not yet transformed. However, if a teammate continues to break a Work Agreement, the team should have an agreed-upon condition within their Agreement that clarifies how they will confront one another. This is the interlocking accountability condition created in Step 9.

Key Work Agreement Facilitation Questions

Work Agreement facilitators ask helpful questions before and during the workshop. Use the below resource to encourage and support your team through each of the 10 Steps.

1. Agree on the first teamwork topic.	*What teamwork issue do you want to address in the workshop? What would be your desired outcome?*
2. Create the topic's desired outcome.	*If our team failed to discuss and agree on how to improve [desired outcome], what would go wrong?* Answers to this question will help you and the team leader to create preventions and interventions.
3. Design an opening question.	*If the team was doing/achieving the desired outcome, what behaviors would we see or hear teammates doing?*
4. Ask the opening question.	For example, *If we communicated respectfully, what would you see or hear teammates say or do, or not say or do?*
5. Capture behavioral answers.	Ask clarifying questions to make sure you are not interpreting answers.
6. Propose an intention statement.	What is the team's overarching intention? What behavior would most of them agree to keep, and would it provide a context for the other behaviors?
7. Ask if it will work.	*If all of you really and truly lived this Work Agreement Intention, would it resolve your issue?*

8. Write clarifications or conditions for acceptance statements.	Use only one or two of these questions. A. *Is this intention practical and doable in your work environment?* B. *What would prevent you from doing/living this intention 100% of the time?* C. *Is there a time, situation, or condition when this intention would not work?* D. *Is there any situation where you would not feel safe keeping this Work Agreement?* E. *What internal or external constraints would get in the way of keeping this Agreement?* F. *Is there anything or anyone that would prevent you from keeping this Agreement?* G. *Is this a clear intention or Agreement? Does anything need editing?* H. *Is everyone clear about what behavior is expected of each teammate?* I. *What do you think? Is this Work Agreement complete? Do you believe everyone understands what we're all agreeing to do?*
9. Create interlocking accountability.	*If someone continues to break this Work Agreement, we will...*
10. Ask them if they will live it.	*Will this Work Agreement succeed, and will you keep this Agreement going forward?*

Facilitating Work Agreements – A Graphic Illustration

Now that we have reviewed the 10 Steps briefly, it's time to go a little deeper. The following illustration of the 10 Steps specifically shows the evolutionary process of transforming your notepad flipcharts into a Work Agreement during the workshop.

Steps 4 & 5

You are in your team workshop. You've asked the opening question, *"If we communicated respectfully, what would you see or hear teammates say or do, or not say or do?"*

When you first start facilitating Work Agreements, consider writing your topic (in this case, "Respectful Communication") on the top of the notepad flipchart, plus your opening question. When you become more experienced, you may stop that practice. For this illustration, the complete list of the team's answers is included here. It will likely take approximately 30 minutes of discussion to generate and capture a list of 12 answers.

Respectful Communication

"If we communicated respectfully, what would you see or hear team members say or do...or not say or do?"

Team Note Pad

1. Ask to interrupt.
2. Be on time for meetings.
3. When disagreeing, use facts to challenge or counter argue.
4. Stop talking behind backs
5. Share information; don't withhold
6. Good communication = good tone of voice & body language and choosing the right words.
7. Give constructive feedback, but in private.
8. If we hear/see others in conflict, we'll step in to help, not avoid.
9. Understand each other's roles.
10. Ask for help if needed.
11. Realize when you are assuming or interpreting.
12. For key decisions, use chain of command.

Step 6

In this step, after the team lists eight to 10 behaviors, you will begin to reflect on their answers. As you do, you will likely see common patterns or themes begin to emerge. **Circle** or **highlight the words** on the notepad flipchart that identify those common themes.

Respectful Communication

"If we communicated respectfully, what would you see or hear team members say or do...or not say or do?"

Team Note Pad

1. Ask to interrupt.
2. Be on time for meetings.
3. When disagreeing, use facts to challenge or counter argue.
4. Stop talking behind backs
5. Share information; don't withhold
6. Good communication = good tone of voice & body language and choosing the right words.
7. Give constructive feedback, but in private.
8. If we hear/see others in conflict, we'll step in to help, not avoid.
9. Understand each other's roles.
10. Ask for help if needed.
11. Realize when you are assuming or interpreting.
12. For key decisions, use chain of command.

These words and concepts will serve as the basis for writing your proposed intention statement.

As you look at those highlighted words, ask yourself:

What is the overarching intention?
What behavior would most of them agree to keep, and would it provide a context for the other behaviors?

Here are some potential intention statements:
- act in a professional way
- communicate in a respectful way with self and the customer
- resolve conflicts respectfully
- give constructive feedback if asked

You choose "communicate in a respectful way" and move to a second flipchart. There, you write your proposed intention statement. When the time is right, you reveal it, saying,

Okay, you've listed 12 ideas for communicating respectfully, any of which could go into your Work Agreement.

I've written an overarching intention statement and included two possible clarifications.

If you like this intention as-is or with some editing, we can finish your Work Agreement by adding more clarifications or conditions for acceptance.

Here's the intention statement: **Each teammate will communicate in a respectful way with each other and our customers.**

Step 7

You ask teammates if they will agree to live the proposed intention. Most of the time, teammates agree. But they usually believe it needs more work. It is still a work in progress.

In our example, many teammates asked to put a period after the word "way." All teammates agreed to this intention with more conditions and clarifications.

Behavioral Agreement – Communication

Intention:

1. Each team member will communicate in a respectful way with each other and our customers.

Clarifications / Conditions for Acceptance:
   A. We will use good communication techniques that include appropriate body language and tone of voice, plus suitable words.
   B. If we see or hear disrespect or we hear an inappropriate behind-back conversation, we own it and need to step in.
   C.

Step 8

In this step, you guide the team in discussing their specific clarifications or conditions for acceptance of the intention statement. As teammates add and edit their conditions, you and the team leader periodically ask them, "If you truly lived your Work Agreement-in-progress, would you achieve your desired outcome?" Most of the time, they will say yes. This "yes" motivates the team to continue making the "right" Agreement for the team.

To facilitate the process of creating clarifications, you can reference the first flipchart with the behavioral descriptions the team has brainstormed, then reframe the behavior into a clarification statement. Share the clarification statement with the team, then ask if they want to include it in their Work Agreement.

For example, after referencing and reframing the sixth idea listed on the flipchart in our example team, you might say,

> *During your discussion over the past half hour, several of you referred to the importance of good communication, so it makes sense to summarize your wish by using the three elements that are included in all communication: words, tone, and body language.*
>
> *The first clarification reads, "We will use good communication techniques that include appropriate body language and tone of voice, plus suitable words."*
>
> *What do you think? Do you want to include these as descriptors of being respectful?*

Pause for a moment to see if you are receiving verbal or nonverbal approval. If teammates agree to this first clarification, draw a line through the sixth idea on the notepad flipchart. Then continue with another behavior, turning it into a clarification statement. For example, with the eighth behavior on the list, you might say:

This clarification combines several suggestions that deal with stepping in and helping others who are in conflict and not withholding. It reads, "If we see or hear disrespect, or we hear inappropriate behind-the-back conversation, we own it and need to step in."

Respectful Communication

"If we communicated respectfully, what would you see or hear team members say or do...or not say or do?"

Team Note Pad

1. Ask to interrupt.
2. Be on time for meetings.
3. When disagreeing, use facts to challenge or counter argue.
4. Stop talking behind backs
5. Share information; don't withhold
6. ~~Good communication = good tone of voice & body language and choosing the right words.~~
7. Give constructive feedback, but in private.
8. ~~If we hear/see others in conflict, we'll step in to help, not avoid.~~
9. Understand each other's roles.
10. Ask for help if needed.
11. Realize when you are assuming or interpreting.
12. For key decisions, use chain of command.

Pause again to see if they agree with the second condition. If they do, draw a line through the eighth behavior on your original notepad flipchart.

Discuss the team's remaining answers and include them (or decide not to include them) in the Work Agreement.

Respectful Communication

"If we communicated respectfully, what would you see or hear team members say or do...or not say or do?"

Team Note Pad

1. Ask to interrupt.
2. Be on time for meetings.
3. When disagreeing, use facts to challenge or counter argue.
4. Stop talking behind backs
5. Share information; don't withhold
6. Good communication = good tone of voice & body language and choosing the right words.
7. Give constructive feedback, but in private.
8. If we hear/see others in conflict, we'll step in to help, not avoid.
9. Understand each other's roles.
10. Ask for help if needed.
11. Realize when you are assuming or interpreting.
12. For key decisions, use chain of command.

Your final Work Agreement should look like this.

Behavioral Agreement – Communication

Team Choice: Intention Statement
1. Each teammate will communicate in a respectful way.

Clarifications / Conditions for Acceptance:

A. We will use good communication techniques that include appropriate body language and tone of voice, plus suitable words.
B. If we see or hear disrespect or we hear inappropriate behind back conversation, we own it and need to step in.
C. If someone unintentionally shows disrespect we will give them the benefit of the doubt, let them know and create a new way to interact going forward.
D. We will actively support team decisions in word, deed and energy; for key decisions we will use our decision-making protocol agreement.
E. We will be on time to meetings.
F. We will ask, "May I interrupt you?"
G. We will use observable facts during disagreements and decision-making and we will acknowledge when we are using assumptions.
H. We will understand each other's roles, ask for help if we need it, share relevant information and if helpful, give constructive feedback in private.
I.

Step 9

This step calls for "interlocking accountability" within the Work Agreement - a vital step to encouraging the team to live their Agreements day in and day out. Fortunately, you will only need to create interlocking accountability once. It will apply to all Work Agreements.

This step will be thoroughly discussed in the upcoming detailed description section.

Behavioral Agreement – Communication

Team Choice: Intention Statement
1. Each teammate will communicate in a respectful way.

Clarifications / Conditions for Acceptance:

A. We will use good communication techniques that include appropriate body language and tone of voice, plus suitable words.
B. If we see or hear disrespect or we hear an inappropriate behind-the-back conversation, we own it and need to step in.
C. If someone unintentionally shows disrespect, we will give them the benefit of the doubt, let them know, and create a new way to interact going forward.
D. We will actively support team decisions in word, deed, and energy; we will use our decision-making protocol agreement for key decisions.
E. We will be on time for meetings.
F. We will ask, "May I interrupt you?"
G. We will use observable facts during disagreements and decision-making, and we will acknowledge when we are using assumptions.
H. We will understand each other's roles, ask for help if we need it, share relevant information and if helpful, give constructive feedback in private.
I. If someone continues to break this agreement, we will tell them that we will invite a third party to help if there is continued disagreement. If that doesn't solve the issues, we will all go to a higher authority for support and resolution.

Step 10

In this step, every teammate publicly commits to hold themselves and others accountable for upholding the team Work Agreement. At this point, everyone should genuinely believe the Agreement will help the team achieve its goals. With the team's affirmative answer, the Work Agreement is complete.

Though it is not a necessary step, sometimes teammates may choose to sign their names as an outward pledge to live their Work Agreement.

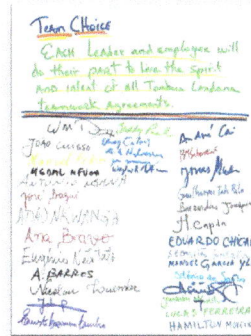

However, posting the Work Agreements where all teammates see them is a good idea.

In this picture, this team posted their three agreements in the hallway. It was a clever and powerful reminder of how they agreed to do no harm and work as one Right-Minded Team.

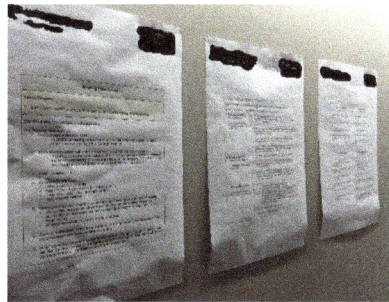

Facilitating Work Agreements – A Detailed Description

Now that we've taken a high-level look at the 10 Steps to facilitating team Work Agreements, let's dive more deeply into the process.

Step 1: Choose a Teamwork Topic that Needs a Team Work Agreement

Any issue that impacts teamwork is suitable for process or behavioral Work Agreements.

Common Work Agreement topics include:
- improving productivity
- clarifying roles
- making better decisions
- increasing trust

There are two methods for identifying teamwork topics:

a. Announce to the team what their first topic will be, or
b. Ask teammates to choose their first topic at the beginning of the team workshop.

There is no one right way to select the first teamwork topic to address, but there are **five essential considerations** to guide you.

Choosing Work Agreement Topics
Five Essential Considerations

The **first consideration** is whether the team is able to communicate positively.

Let's say you are facilitating a team event for a team where the majority of teammates are at odds with one another. They tend to communicate in circles or get stuck in the "attack-defend cycle." If this is the case, it is best to consult teammates for their opinions of what topics the team needs to address. Then, you and the team leader pick the first two topics.

This approach expedites the selection process because, based on the team's poor communication, it could take too much time to ask teammates to collectively choose a topic at the beginning of the workshop.

If you pick the topics, you may also want to implement a prevention (more about preventions in Step 2) by sharing those topics with all teammates several days before the workshop. Doing so will help you gain their active support.

If you and the team leader pre-select the team's workshop topics, here is what you would say at the beginning of the workshop:

> *As you know, the first two topics of this workshop will be about communicating respectfully and decision-making.*
>
> *When we finish creating Work Agreements for those topics, we will brainstorm a list of additional issues to address, and you, as a team, will choose which one to work on next.*

So please, be patient, okay? We will get to all the other topics.
And if we don't finish them today, we'll address them in our next
meeting.

The **second consideration** when choosing Work Agreement topics is
your own comfort level and amount of experience.

If you are a relatively new facilitator, or even if you are an
experienced facilitator who might be a bit unsure about facilitating a
Work Agreements workshop, it is best to pre-select the team's
workshop topics.

Doing so will give you time to mentally prepare and, more
importantly, to craft the right opening question. Designing and
presenting a good opening question is particularly important to the
success of your workshop.

In time, as your facilitation skills improve, you will be able to craft an
opening question on the spot, no matter what topic your team chooses.
And you should aspire to get there because when you can ask the right
question at the right time, teammates will immediately engage.
Speaking their language will make it much easier to guide and
facilitate their discussion. Setting the tone in this way nearly
guarantees their willingness to find solutions.

But it's wise not to expect to demonstrate that level of proficiency in
your first workshop. Instead, choose your topic ahead of time, and
focus on developing a strong opening question. We'll talk more about
how to do this in Step 4, but to give you an idea of what a strong
opening question sounds like, here is a good example:

If we communicated respectfully, what would you see or hear
teammates say or do...or not say or do?

The **third consideration** is whether the team is already bogged down in toxic interpersonal issues, such as a lack of trust or respect.

If this is the case, it is usually best to start with a work process issue instead of a behavioral issue since process topics are typically less emotionally charged. Once the team succeeds in creating and living a good process Work Agreement, the group's emotional toxicity will naturally decrease, creating an "ally atmosphere" for discussing their interpersonal issues.

. . . . .

A True Story

A team of 80 employees worked in a major capital project team. There was a lack of trust among many.

During teammate interviews, it was evident they had too many meetings, and some were not valuable. "Meeting effectiveness," a work process issue, was the topic we chose.

Before the workshop, a small study team was formed. A few days later, they submitted a proposal to reduce and streamline meetings.

In their first Work Agreements workshop, their plan was reviewed, discussed, modified, and agreed upon by all teammates.

Their process Work Agreement mapped out how they would use agendas, desired outcomes, and ground rules in their meetings. It also covered how to speak up if a meeting got off-track. The "how to speak up" condition was primarily a promise to forgive each other (a Reason-based attitude) in future sessions, if necessary. That one condition of the Work Agreement almost guaranteed they would recover, restore themselves to their collective Right Mind, and get back on track, no matter what happened during their meetings.

Several of the stipulations in their Work Agreement were beautifully aligned with RMT's Top 10 To-Dos for Successful Meetings, which can be found in the Resources section below.

After one month, teammates reported getting more work done because they were not in so many meetings. Plus, the meetings they did have were better organized and facilitated.

The team unanimously declared the Work Agreement a success, and the team leader estimated **they saved $10,000 (USD) a week in labor costs.**

Every teammate benefited. It was a quick win, one which created genuine motivation and willingness to continue improving teamwork and addressing further team issues like trust and respect.

. . . . .

The **fourth consideration** is deciding how you want to help teammates identify workshop topics.

There are two methods: interviews and surveys.

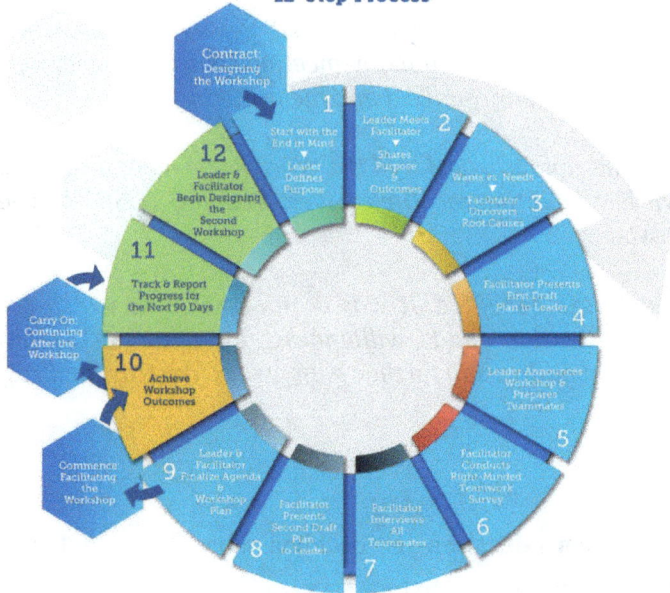

How to Design a
Right-Minded
TEAMWORK
Team-Building Workshop:
12-Step Process

Interviewing teammates is the most effective option.

Team interviews are so effective they are also explained thoroughly in another RMT book, ***Design a Right-Minded, Team-Building Workshop***: *12 Steps to Create a Team That Works as One.*

See Step 7.

Based on your teammate interviews, it will be easy to identify several topics that most teammates will want to resolve.

Conducting **teammate surveys** is the other way to identify workshop topics. There are many surveys available on the market today; for a Right-Minded Teamwork survey specifically designed to elicit possible topics for Work Agreements workshops, try RMT's *Team Perception Survey.*

Additionally, you could use RMT's *9 Right Choices Survey* or RMT's *Team Performance Factor Assessment.*

Whether you choose to interview teammates or send out a survey, list all the proposed topics your team suggests in a Punch List. Include a copy of that list with the Team Work Agreements Workshop Agenda. You will find a real agenda and Punch List as an example in the Resources section below.

The **fifth consideration** for picking a topic relates to identifying external issues affecting the team.

Many organizations require their work teams to comply with initiatives and programs like workplace safety, diversity, ethics, and behavioral values. These critical issues are "external" to the team.

Let's look at organizational values to better understand this consideration. Values such as trust, respect, and accountability are typical company values. Teammates readily embrace such values, but teammates will always have different interpretations of exactly what those values mean.

Take respect, for example. One teammate may think being consistently late for meetings is disrespectful, and yet another teammate may think interrupting others before they've finished talking is disrespectful. Neither is necessarily right or wrong, but the discrepancy in their opinions can cause conflict.

When teammates openly discuss and agree on what being respectful means to them, they are able to create a transparent Work Agreement that defines respect for the team as a whole, in behavioral terms. Their Work Agreement is uniquely suited to the team, and because everyone is on the same page and not in conflict, the Agreement also helps ensure the team is aligned with the organization's values.

Summary

By considering your team's ability to communicate positively, their current level of interpersonal conflict, your own level of facilitation experience, the best approach for understanding what the team hopes to gain or resolve in their workshop, and any external issues affecting them, you will find the right topic for their first Work Agreements workshop.

Remember, no matter which method you use to identify topics, it is imperative to understand the issues *from the teammates' point of view and the outcomes they want to achieve.*

That is not to say teammates' points of view are accurate. It also doesn't mean what they say they *want* is truly what they *need.*

> *It is essential for you, as their facilitator, to understand where **they currently think they are** so you can help them create a **roadmap to get to where they need to go**.*

To do so, you will need to set aside your ideas about the best topics for the team, at least during teammate interviews, so you can really listen to and hear issues from their point of view. Understanding *their* view of *their* topic and *why it matters to them* will make it relatively easy to write desired outcomes that teammates can't wait to address in their workshop.

When you ensure your teammates feel understood and heard, you are doing your part to help them move into their collective Right Mind.

Step 2: Determine Your Teamwork Topic's Desired Outcome

Once you have selected the first topic to address in your Work Agreements workshop, it is time to clarify your desired outcome for the workshop. There are two practical reasons for doing so.

Firstly, the desired outcome is a key component of your workshop agenda. It defines the result or product teammates will aim to accomplish by the end of the workshop. In our case, the product is a Work Agreement about decision-making and communicating respectfully.

Secondly, identifying your outcome ensures teammates address the *cause* (behavior) behind the problem and not just the *effect* (respect or lack of respect).

Let's say you hear in the teammate interviews they want to see more respect among one another. When you ask what behaviors are causing the disrespect, you hear that people are consistently late for meetings, many people interrupt others before they have finished talking, and that too many teammates don't complete their work tasks on time.

Therefore, communicating respectfully is an appropriate chosen topic. But the solution - their Work Agreement - will outline new, specific *behaviors* - being on time, minimizing interruptions, and getting work done on time - that, when followed, actually address the root cause of the problem.

As discussed before, it is critical that you understand the topic *from your teammates' point of view* and *why it matters to them*. Both are key to creating *a workshop outcome they want and need to achieve*.

When creating a process-oriented outcome, it is helpful to imagine the team writing a procedure or set of instructions. Here is a good example of a work process outcome:

Discuss and agree on our team's decision-making protocol.

When creating a behavioral outcome, think in terms of identifying the behaviors people will demonstrate to achieve the result. In our case, here is the outcome we created:

Discuss and agree on our team's accepted communication practices.

Three Rules About Specificity

The teamwork topic's desired outcome also needs to indicate how detailed the team's Work Agreements should be. This means you will make some assumptions for each team you facilitate about how specific their Agreements need to be.

Here are three rules to guide you:

1. Never create an Agreement written so broadly it only addresses the effect.
2. Never create an Agreement so detailed and specific that it tries to resolve the team's issue's subatomic root cause.
3. Create an Agreement that lands between rule one and rule two.

Let's use the decision-making process example above to bring more light to these rules.

Our desired outcome is to *discuss and agree on a team decision-making protocol.*

Let's say after some group conversation, the team decided on the following intention statement for their Work Agreement: *Everyone will have the opportunity to contribute to team decisions*.

This Agreement breaks rule one because it is not specific enough. It feels open-ended and vague, like a halfhearted attempt to address the issue of decision-making.

Let's say the team created this intention statement: *For technical decisions, teammates with graduate degrees in mechanical, electrical, or computer engineering will make the final decision.*

This Agreement breaks rule two because it is too specific. It is also divisive because it makes the false assumption that certain people are better qualified to make team decisions than others.

Now, let's say the team created the following intention statement: *For all critical team decisions, we will go for consensus, but if we cannot come to a consensus, our fallback will be for Maria [the team leader] to decide.*

This process Work Agreement intention statement satisfies rule three, giving enough specificity without being too detailed. Once the team adds conditions and clarifications, it will be exactly right for this team. In Step 8, you will learn how to facilitate the discussion around those clarifications and conditions for acceptance.

Share the Desired Outcome

Now, let's imagine you're in the workshop. The leader has welcomed everyone and has turned the facilitation duties over to you.

You have acknowledged the two topics on the agenda: communicating respectfully and decision-making. Now, the team is ready to address the first topic.

To begin the conversation, as the facilitator, you say:

> *As you know, one of the topics we agreed to address was respect.*
>
> *With that in mind, the desired outcome for this topic is to "discuss and agree on our team's accepted communication practices."*
>
> *If today you create a Work Agreement that you believe will achieve that outcome, and starting tomorrow, you all begin to live it, would you increase respect for one another?*

Their answer will always be yes, setting you up for your opening question and the team's discussion.

Before we move to Step 3, asking the opening question, let's discuss two additional workshop components: Preventions & Interventions and Decision-Making Work Agreements.

Preventions & Interventions

Before the workshop, you and the team leader must identify barriers that could inhibit teammates from creating strong Work Agreements.

That discussion will lead you both to create preventions that will, hopefully, prevent those issues from occurring during your workshop.

However, if your preventions don't work, you also need to agree on how you will intervene.

For example, let's say there is a resistant teammate who doesn't like team building because of several bad experiences.

As a prevention, you will actively engage that teammate in designing the workshop. Hopefully, they will offer good ideas that you can incorporate into the plan. When they see their opinions have made it into the final list, they will feel validated and heard. Often, this recognition naturally leads to engagement. When it does, the prevention of engaging the resistant teammate in the design process can be deemed effective.

If the teammate does not engage or becomes resistant during the workshop, the pre-planned intervention might be for you and the leader to talk privately with the teammate during a break.

Identify Workshop Barriers

On any team, two types of barriers may arise during a workshop:
1. Process barriers
2. People barriers

Depending on the team and the barrier, these barriers can show up as minor nuisances or significant problems.

Examples of process barriers:

- An interdependent virtual team is divided into four time zones.
- Because of shift work, not all teammates can attend the workshop.
- Too many layers of management approval slow down processing.

Examples of people barriers:

- The team struggles with language or cultural differences.
- A teammate resists team building.
- There is toxic and unresolved conflict between teammates.

Most workshops will have around three to five barriers. As you consider your team's barriers, remember your team leader knows their teammates better than you do.

Ask the leader:

- What could go wrong in the workshop?
- How can we prevent those wrongs/barriers from happening?
- How will we intervene if they happen?

For each barrier you identify, you and the team leader will create a prevention-intervention plan.

This conversation often starts way back in Step 2 of the 12 Steps when you learn about the leader's desired outcomes.

When the workshop agenda is complete in Step 9, you and the leader need to finish planning your preventions and interventions. For each barrier you identify, you two will create a prevention-intervention plan.

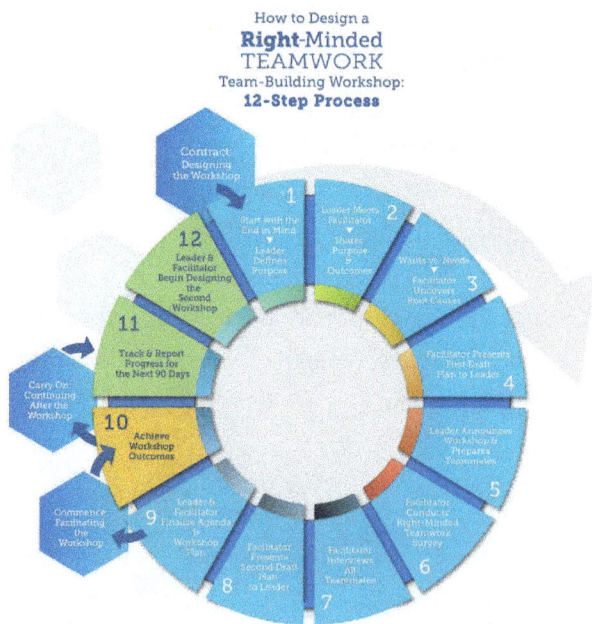

How to Design a
Right-Minded
TEAMWORK
Team-Building Workshop:
12-Step Process

Create a Prevention Plan

Two examples of preventative measures you can take to address a resistant teammate are **inclusion** and a **pre-workshop agreement**.

In the planning phase, inclusion means you will genuinely interview the opposing teammate, ensuring that the teammate knows their workshop design ideas are equally as crucial as those of their fellow teammates. Share with them that it is essential for all teammates, including them, to believe the final workshop outcomes are worthwhile. Every teammate must be committed to achieving them for the team to succeed.

After the team leader approves the final agenda, inclusion means returning to the resistant teammate and walking through the agenda with them. Your goal is to give them a chance to get on board and embrace the workshop outcomes' benefits.

After reviewing the outcomes with them, ask,

> *Do you agree that if we accomplished these workshop outcomes, our team-building efforts would have been worth it?*

When the teammate says yes (even if their response is not very convincing!), affirm them. Tell them,

> *That's great news. It's important you believe that. I'm counting on you to do everything you can to make certain we have a good workshop. Can I count on you?*

With their consent, you've made a pre-workshop agreement and a pretty solid prevention plan. Of course, the next question to consider is, how will you intervene if this teammate becomes negative in the workshop despite your agreement?

Create an Intervention Plan

To assist in handling interventions, follow **PCA**, a facilitator tool that means Present, Clarify, and Agree. You should use this tool at the beginning of every team-building workshop.

Present

- Kick off the meeting by presenting the workshop outcomes, agenda, and ground rules.

Clarify

- Ask teammates if they have any clarifying questions. When you ask, be sure to pause; don't say anything for a short while.

- Typically, there are no questions because you have distributed the agenda ahead of time and have discussed it with any resistant teammates.

- Occasionally, someone may ask a simple question or add a new ground rule like, *It's okay to disagree, but it's not okay to be disrespectful or negative.*

Agree

- While you are waiting for questions, look into everyone's eyes. Do you see acceptance?

  If you do see acceptance on people's faces, say,

- *Okay. It looks like everyone understands the outcomes and agrees to abide by the ground rules and Decision-Making Agreement. Does everyone agree to do their part today?*

Everyone says yes, and you're ready to move on.

Escalating Interventions

Even the best-planned workshops sometimes go sideways. It's essential to know how to intervene if things happen to go astray. When intervening, use an escalating intervention approach.

Always use the lowest level of intervention first.

Only escalate to a higher-level intervention if the previous intervention does not work.

Lower-level interventions:

- If a teammate becomes negative in the workshop, remind them of the outcomes and the agreed-upon ground rules.

- Gently interrupt a tangent or escalating situation by "boomeranging" the non-stop talker's idea by asking another participant to comment on that idea.

- If there is a disruptive sidebar conversation that continues, slowly move towards the chatty teammates without saying a word. Often your presence alone will correct behavior.

Mid-level interventions:

- Reflect on what you are seeing or hearing in the room without judgment. Say, *I see /hear* _____. *What's going on?*

- If someone says something off-topic or not useful, find a portion of their statement you can accept and legitimize. Then either address their off-topic question or ask for permission to defer the topic to the holding bin.

- If appropriate, use humor. But proceed with caution. Never make fun of anyone.

High-level interventions:

- When there's a conflict or misunderstanding, ask the people in conflict to state the other's point of view to ensure mutual understanding.

- Take a break and talk with the agitated or disruptive person(s) offline. Taking time to understand their concerns can help create a way to get them back into collaboration.

- Confront the group or the people in conflict with the behavior you are seeing and hearing. Ask for ideas to resolve it.

Learning how to create and implement preventions and interventions is not hard, but addressing conflict can initially be uncomfortable. However, it is part of your role as a facilitator. Like other team-building skills, you will get better and better at it the more you practice.

Step 3: Design Your Opening Question

Now that you know your desired outcomes, the next step is to create an opening question that sets a positive tone and kicks off your workshop's topic discussion.

Asking good questions is an important skill, one worth practicing and learning. Two excellent books on the subject are:

- *Making Questions Work: A Guide to How and What to Ask for Facilitators, Consultants, Managers, Coaches and Educators* by Dorothy Strachan

- *The Secrets of Facilitation: The S.M.A.R.T. Guide to Getting Results with Groups* by Michael Wilkinson (focused on what he calls A and B questions)

In addition to what these authors can teach you, there are **two extremely critical construction techniques** you will need to apply when designing an opening question:

1. Aim to create **accountability-based** questions instead of brainstorm-based questions.

2. Ask *"what"* questions more often than *"why"* questions.

Accountability-Based Questions

What would happen if I asked a question such as, *Why were some teams more successful in demonstrating respect?* You might hear answers like; *People didn't take things so seriously.*

This is a good brainstorming question. But it is not a good Work Agreement question. It does not oblige participants to declare what they will commit to demonstrating in their team right now.

For Work Agreement workshops, it's far more effective to help participants get into and stay in a commitment mindset by crafting accountability-based questions such as:

If we communicated respectfully, what would you see or hear teammates say or do, or not say or do?

If we respected one another at the highest level, what would you see teammates do or say to one another?

When people show you respect, what behaviors are you seeing or hearing?

What should we start, stop, or continue doing to ensure our team makes good decisions?

The first three questions are excellent accountability-based questions for *interpersonal* desired outcomes. The fourth question is an excellent accountability-based question for a *process* outcome.

Note the question structure used in the first three behavioral questions. You can follow the same format and use it for designing opening questions for behavioral Work Agreements:

If we did _____ *(the topic or outcome),* **what would we see or hear teammates do or say** *(behaviors)?*

Accountability-based questions formulated in this way force participants to talk about what *they* want or need.

This type of question also keeps participants focused on resolving their issues, whereas brainstorm questions often create conversational and perhaps irrelevant tangents.

As the facilitator, be vigilant in monitoring the team's dialogue. If the conversation strays into an intellectual or noncommittal brainstorm, gently interrupt, and bring them back to how *they* will commit to working together going forward.

By asking accountability-based questions, you help teammates personalize their answers, which is a beautiful gift to give them. You are helping surface and make visible what truly matters to them.

If you accidentally ask a brainstorm question when you meant to ask an accountability question, that's okay. Just acknowledge it, and then ask the correct question. Here's an example:

> *Okay, why do you think other teams have been able to demonstrate respect more successfully in the past?*

As soon as you realize you misspoke, back up, and rephrase:

> *Oops! I meant to ask if you were communicating respectfully with one another, what would you see or hear teammates say or do?*

What vs. Why Questions

Asking what questions versus why questions are just as important as crafting accountability-based questions. What's the difference?

- A *what* question is more about the *future*. A *why* question is more about the *past*.
- A *what* question leans towards *accountability*. A *why* question leans towards *victimization*.
- An example of a *what* question is, *What do you want me to do differently going forward?*
- An example of a *why* question is, *Why did you do that?* …which usually sounds judgmental.

To be clear, *why* questions are not always wrong. If the team is relatively functional and has a willingness to correct its mistakes versus punishing teammates, asking why may be beneficial.

But if the team is dysfunctional, asking why could sound like a dysfunctional parent-child conversation, like this:

Parent: *Please go clean up your room before you go out to play*.
Child: *Why?*

Parent: *Because it's messy*.
Child: *Why?*

Parent: *Because you messed it up!*
Child: *Why?*

Parent: *Because you are a slob!!*
Child: *Why?*

Parent: *Because it's in your DNA! Your dad/mom is a slob, and you are, too!*

No one leaves that conversation feeling good. A parent-child conversation is not helpful in team building. Asking *what* instead will help your teammates create better Work Agreements.

What questions force respondents to offer practical solutions that can be turned into effective, transformative Work Agreements.

Step 4: Ask the Opening Question

Imagine you are now 10 minutes into the workshop. The team leader has already welcomed everyone. All teammates have agreed to the meeting's outcomes, agenda, ground rules, and the day's logistics.

Before you ask your opening question, take five minutes to introduce Right-Minded Teamwork's Right Choice Model. This will establish a positive, do-no-harm, work-as-one atmosphere for the remainder of the workshop.

Your goal is to present the Right Choice Model in such a way that when you finish, all teammates declare,

> *Of course, we need to approach [our issue] in a Right-Minded, accountable way. Let's get started.*

Another option is for the team leader to present the Right Choice Model by relating it to a current difficult team challenge.

Either way, after you present the Model, and the team's collective "Decision-Maker" has committed to a Right-Minded approach, ***it is time for you to ask the opening question.***

To Learn More...

To learn more about the Right Choice Model and how to apply it in your team, go to RightMindedTeamwork.com or your favorite book retailer, and pick up ***How to Apply the Right Choice Model***: *Create a Right-Minded Team That Works as One.* Within the book, look for the section titled, "How to Present & Apply the Right Choice Model in Your Team."

There, you will be given specific instructions on successfully presenting the Right Choice Model, including how to relate it to your team's current challenge.

Asking the opening question is Step 4 in the 10 Steps to facilitating team Work Agreements, and it officially starts the team's honest discussion on the first teamwork topic.

Up to this point, you have been doing most of the talking. However, after you ask the opening question, you will shift to listening, observing, and facilitating for the remainder of the workshop.

When Is the Right Time to Ask the Opening Question?

It is important to ask your opening question at the right moment. You will know it is the right time when:

- You believe participants are clear about the topic's desired outcome and will abide by the workshop's ground rules.

- You believe they are ready and willing to engage.

Just before asking the opening question, you could say something like:

> *I'm going to ask a question to get our conversation started, and I encourage you to share each answer in such a way that it sounds like a commitment—a commitment you would be willing to keep.*

This last-minute lead-in is an attempt to prevent a brainstorm or, worse still, a victim-type answer such as, *I think if management stopped pitting us against each other, we could learn to respect each other.*

If a teammate makes a statement like that, you will need to transform that energy by encouraging the group to make statements that describe what *they* will do to make things better, not what they think others outside the group should do.

That's not to say the group should never talk about others outside the team. But if they do, the conversation needs to be about what teammates will do to influence others.

If the conversation derails into a brainstorm or victim answers, you may need to say something like:

> *Please remember that your Work Agreements are about what you will do going forward, not what others will do.*

For Steps 4-10 of this book, we will use this opening question as our example:

> *If we communicated respectfully, what would you see or hear teammates say or do, or not say or do?*

Step 5: Capture Teammate Answers

Now that you've asked the opening question, it's time to listen, observe, think, and capture the team's legitimate ideas on a flipchart, all at the same time. Sounds challenging, doesn't it? It can be, but it is a learnable skill.

Overview

Step 5 is an essential step with a lot of detailed instructions. First, here's a high-level summary of how this step works and how it fits with the next three steps.

- You've asked the opening question in **Step 4**, and teammates begin to answer.

- In **Step 5**, you are at the flipchart capturing their legitimate ideas. Think of this flipchart as the team's visual notepad. Soon you will use another flipchart to begin writing an intention statement, which is **Step 6.**

- When the intention statement is agreed upon in **Step 7,** you will go to the chart and scratch off the answers that were used to create the intention.

- In **Step 8**, the remaining items on the notepad are transformed and transferred onto the second flipchart as clarifications or conditions for accepting the new Work Agreement.

Respectful Communication

"If we communicated respectfully, what would you see or hear team members say or do...or not say or do?"

Team Note Pad

1. Ask to interrupt.
2. Be on time for meetings.
3. When disagreeing, use facts to challenge or counter argue.
4. Stop talking behind backs
5. Share information; don't withhold
6. ~~Good communication = good tone of voice & body language and choosing the right words.~~
7. Give constructive feedback, but in private.
8. ~~If we hear/see others in conflict, we'll step in to help, not avoid.~~
9. Understand each other's roles.
10. Ask for help if needed.
11. Realize when you are assuming or interpreting.
12. For key decisions, use chain of command.

Visual Notepad; Work-in-Progress

There are two essential skills to apply in this step:

1. Recognize and capture legitimate behavioral answers.

2. Recognize and know how to use both a simple and a complex answer.

Recognizing & Capturing Legitimate Behavioral Answers

It's easy to assume that everyone understands what behavior is. Still, many times, especially during tense conversations, teammates may not even be aware that they are using non-behavioral terms.

What is behavior?

In the simplest of terms, behavior is something you see someone do or hear someone say. But behavior is also what someone does *not* do or does *not* say. You might call these *avoidance behaviors*.

To become a master Work Agreements facilitator, you must understand behaviors and develop a keen sense of which behaviors are legitimate and which are not. This is because behavioral statements are the building blocks of all Work Agreements.

You will also need to be able to teach what behaviors are and are not in a swift and concise training module.

What makes a behavior legitimate?

If the core behavior within a teammate's answer to your opening question helps teammates resolve their issues and achieve their desired outcome, you have heard a legitimate response.

While you are facilitating, there will be times when someone will use vague concepts instead of communicating a specific behavior their teammates could easily see or hear.

For example, if a teammate says, *Joe and Kelly have bad attitudes,* are they describing behavior? No. They're stating a judgment, which is only a vague description, even though it is meaningful to them.

Is it okay to use vague terms? Yes, in everyday work conversation. But it's not helpful during an Agreements workshop. Vague pronouncements like "bad attitude" increase the likelihood of the conversation degrading into an argument. Plus, vagueness wastes time because those descriptions are too imprecise to be helpful.

When you hear a vague answer that could have legitimately associated behaviors, you will be faced with an immediate choice: You can either ask the person to define the behaviors that describe their suggestion, or you can seize the opportunity to conduct a two-minute teaching module for the entire group on behaviors.

As the facilitator, you need to watch and listen carefully for those times when participants need to speak in behavioral terms. Be ready to gently step in to redirect or help if they don't self-correct.

Here's an example. Let's say you are facilitating a meeting of department leaders and their boss.

One leader, in a frustrated tone of voice, says,

> *I'm really disappointed in the lack of respect some departments have for other departments. I think we need an Agreement about showing respect!*

Can you see how nonspecific this statement is? The term *respect* is relative. Respect means different behaviors to different people.

By the way, this is one of those statements in which the speaker likely does not realize they have just communicated a vague message. Typically, they don't recognize it because they are in an emotional, wrong-minded attitude instead of a rational, Right-Minded attitude.

Hearing this challenging statement, it's possible other leaders in the meeting are silently reacting, getting ready to attack or defend. Or, they might be preparing a comment to satisfy the speaker or steer the conversation to a less confrontational topic.

As the facilitator, you will need to make an immediate decision to either step into the conversation or wait to see if another teammate will respond.

If you decide to step in and intervene, you could ask:

> *Would you give us a behavioral example that leads you to believe there is a lack of department respect?*

If the emotional department leader can successfully describe "lack of respect" behaviors, you could also ask them to explain actions that *would* indicate respect. Whether you agree with them or not, you would capture their suggestions, which are now legitimate behaviors, on the notepad before continuing to facilitate the discussion.

Now let's pretend another teammate quickly responded to the emotional leader. The first leader says,

> *I'm really disappointed in the lack of respect some departments have for other departments. I think we need an Agreement about showing respect!*

Another leader responds,

> *If you're referencing what I said yesterday about your department, that's not showing disrespect. That was a legitimate challenge to your department's productivity. You just want to have your hand in other people's departments. You have enough to do without meddling in my department's affairs.*

The two leaders' bodies lean forward, and they begin to stare at each other. Their tones of voice rise.

These signals mean it is time for you to intervene. No matter what, as the facilitator, you have to help this team turn around this attack-defend conversational style.

Remember our discussion of Preventions & Interventions? This is one of those times you will be glad you and the team leader discussed and agreed on your intervention plans. Now that the time has come, you begin with low-level interventions. You might move your body so you are somewhat in between the conflicting teammates. Or, you could interrupt and remind them they agreed to find solutions at the beginning of the meeting, not to blame one another.

When this kind of conversation happens, it is not always bad, but if it goes on too long, the Work Agreements workshop will likely fail. Said another way, when people argue like this, they are stuck in an adversarial mode. The longer you allow a group to stay in that emotional, wrong-minded, ego-driven space, the harder it becomes to move them into a Right-Minded, Reason-based, ally-focused conversation.

In a situation like this, another important thing to note is how fixed the adversaries are in their interpretation of what respect means.

Now let's take a look at another example of a possible teammate interaction. The emotional team leader says,

> *I'm really disappointed in the lack of respect some departments have for other departments. I think we need an Agreement about showing respect!*

Another leader responds,

> *I think I agree with you because we all want and deserve respect. But I'm not sure what you are seeing or hearing that leads you to this conclusion. Would you give us an example?*

If you hear a comment like this, don't say anything. Stay out of the way and go with the flow. The team is already seeking legitimate behavioral answers. When the time is right, compliment and positively praise the team for their self-facilitation. And, as always, capture all new, legitimate, behavioral answers on the flipchart.

As a master facilitator, when it comes to recognizing and capturing legitimate behaviors, you must develop a keen sense of work behaviors for two reasons:

1. In successful Work Agreement workshops, the majority of the time is spent identifying and agreeing on a set of behaviors teammates will demonstrate going forward. Therefore, as the facilitator, your job is to help ensure they use the language of behaviors (what one sees or hears).

2. These behaviors are written down and captured because they will be reviewed periodically and even fine-tuned in future team-building meetings.

In short, you must know a behavior when you see or hear one. You must also master the art of listening to 10 or 15 people without interpreting or judging their messages. Only then can you effectively facilitate *and* capture the behaviors that will work best in their Work Agreements.

Is it okay to have some non-behavioral concepts in your Work Agreement? Yes, as long as that is not all there is.

Imagine a Work Agreement with only vague terms. Initially, it might seem all right, but it would not be useful as a daily tool because of all the potential misinterpretations that would result.

If you look at the example Work Agreements in this book, you will see some vague terms. But you will also see specific behaviors outlined in each Agreement.

Simple or Complex Answers

As you become more adept at recognizing legitimate behaviors, you will begin to notice different types of behavioral answers. Most responses can be mentally categorized, in real-time, as either a *simple* or *complex* answer.

A simple answer might sound like this:

> *As your leader, I want to keep my open-door policy, but I need to limit the number of interruptions I get during the day because I'm so busy. For me, respect would mean that you would ask if I can respond then when you interrupt. If I would rather stay focused on my current task, I'll request to get back to you.*

This answer is *simple* because it appears to have an uncomplicated solution.

A *complex* answer from another teammate might sound like:

> *In my culture, we show respect for our elders and leaders. It is not appropriate or acceptable to challenge an elder's decision, so, for me, respect means that I will do what my boss wants me to do.*

This statement was an actual comment from a teammate in a multicultural, international team. This answer is *complex* because it contains many divergent elements and belief patterns around culture, age, and role ambiguity. There is even a slight undercurrent of fear.

Are complex answers more difficult to facilitate than simple answers? Due to their complexity, they can be. However, the simple answer is not necessarily easier to facilitate. Simple answers sometimes are solutions for symptoms. They may fail to resolve a much deeper, unspoken problem.

Remember, the concept of simple and complex answers is intended as a thinking tool for you, the facilitator. Please do not tell participants that their solutions are "simple" or label your flipcharts with these terms. Simple versus complex is a conceptual distinction that will help you organize and analyze teammates' answers in real-time, thus helping you formulate a proper response.

Whether their answers are simple or complex, your goal is still the same: help teammates identify and capture legitimate behaviors they believe will help their team achieve the topic's desired outcome. On a broader scale, you are also helping the team describe the attitudes and behaviors they think will help them create and sustain Right-Minded Teamwork, thus achieving 100% customer satisfaction.

Step 6: Write & Propose an Intention Statement

By the end of this step, you will understand how to deliver your intention statement and present the start of an Agreement - the initial intention statement.

Using what you believe is the team's most practical idea, you will write and propose an intention statement that starts with:

Each teammate will...

When you're ready to present your proposed intention statement, you will say:

Okay, you've listed 12 ideas for communicating respectfully which might go into your Work Agreement. I've written an overarching intention statement and included two possible conditions for acceptance.

If you like this intention as it is or with some editing, we can finish your Work Agreement by adding more clarifications and conditions.

The intention is: "Each teammate will communicate in a respectful way with each other and our customers."

Multitasking

You must multitask while facilitating Work Agreements.

From the moment you ask the opening question and begin capturing the team's behaviors, you must mentally and physically multitask. Most people struggle at first, but you will improve with practice, and soon these facilitation techniques will become second nature.

During Steps 5 and 6 of facilitating your Work Agreements workshop, you will:

- **Listen** carefully to understand and capture legitimate behaviors that summarize the team's answers to your opening question.

- **Observe** teammate's body language as they listen to others.

- **Analyze** the legitimate behaviors you have captured.

- **Identify** the team's most practical ideas.

- **Write** and **propose** an intention statement.

We will talk about each of these activities separately but recognize they are all taking place simultaneously in your mind while you are facilitating.

Listen to Understand

Listening to understand is necessary for capturing legitimate ideas. You must be able to capture *their ideas* without filtering or interpreting them when you write them on the flipchart. Occasionally, there are times when a person is trying hard to offer a legitimate solution but is struggling to find the right words; when that happens, it is okay for you to reflect on what you think they are saying to give them a few precise behavioral terms. Generally, though, you want to retain their language on your flipcharts whenever possible.

You may be wondering how much time you should allow for capturing their ideas and writing the intention statement. It's difficult to give an exact answer, but 15 minutes is probably too short, and 45 minutes is usually too long. Only one thing is sure: A team's first Work Agreement always takes longer than the second Agreement.

If it is the team's first Work Agreement, I recommend allowing enough time to list 10 to 15 ideas, which might take 30 minutes. By allowing more time for the team's first Work Agreement, you establish a focused and positive atmosphere in which people actively move towards creating valuable Agreements.

When you help the team achieve a positive, problem-solving conversational style, you will use more steering-type facilitation techniques, guiding their conversation rather than driving it.

In the past, some people have asked if they could just facilitate and have someone else capture the answers on the flipchart. The answer is yes, you can, but I highly recommend you learn to do both at the same time. Introducing a scribe can be distracting for both you and the team, especially since you and your recorder are unlikely to hear teammates' ideas in precisely the same way. If you decide to use a scribe, a good rule would be for the recorder to look to you for the right words to capture, rather than directly engaging with the team.

Observe Physical Responses

There are two subtle observation skills you will want to use throughout the workshop.

1. Watch the current participant's eyes.

If you have asked a question and the person who responds looks directly at you and does not look at other teammates while they are giving their answer, move out of their line of sight so that it covertly causes them to look at and speak to others.

2. Observe the body language of those who are listening.

Observing means watching teammates' eyes and body movements when they are listening to other teammates' answers. Observe their physical, and nonverbal behaviors while listening to the speaker, such as leaning in or shaking their head.

A Reason-able Idea…
Facilitate Work Agreements workshops in a way that ensures teammates look at and talk to each other 90% of the time, rather than talking to you, the facilitator.

Much of our body language is unconscious but fairly obvious. If you see someone smiling, they likely agree with the speaker. If you see teammates rolling their eyes and frowning, then you can assume, at least for the moment, that the teammate likely disagrees with the speaker.

By observing listeners, you are, in essence, reading the energy in the room, or at least your interpretation of that energy. It is okay to interpret body language, but please do not assume your interpretations are necessarily accurate. It's wise to have a healthy skepticism about your own judgments.

Once I observed a listener who threw his head back, with his arms over his head, and rolled his eyes. Based on his behavior, I concluded he disagreed with his fellow teammate.

When the teammate finished talking, I asked that particular listener to put his reaction into words to check my interpretation.

Much to my surprise, he said emphatically,

> *Oh, yes! I couldn't agree with him more! He's totally correct.*

My interpretation of his body language was completely wrong. He was agreeing, not disagreeing.

A Reason-able Idea…
When in doubt, check it out! Don't assume you can *accurately read body language.*

Analyze Behaviors

From the moment you ask your opening question, you will be analyzing what you are seeing and hearing in the workshop.

There are **three interrelated things to analyze**:

1. **Nonverbal behavior**
   By watching group body language as you listen to the team conversation, you will be able to determine if the overall discussion is moving towards collective agreement or disagreement.

2. **Answers that are not quite legitimate behaviors**
   If you think an answer is too vague but could be legitimate, ask the group to assist. Many times, the group will build off a response and create a legitimate behavioral answer.

3. **When to begin formulating the intention statement**
   There is no set rule on when to start developing your proposed intention statement, but usually, you can start when you have between eight and 10 legitimate behaviors listed.

Here is a simple and powerful technique that makes a working analysis visible to the group and helps converge the list towards an intention statement.

After the team lists about eight to 10 behaviors, you will likely see common patterns or themes begin to emerge. **Circle** or **highlight the words** on the notepad flipchart that identify those common themes.

These words and concepts will serve as the basis for writing your proposed intention statement.

On this page, you will see the behaviors identified by our real-world example team during their workshop. In their answers, I saw two working themes regarding respectful communication.

The first theme, which can be labeled as *being transparent and open*, was evidenced by #4 (stop talking behind backs) and #5 (share information).

The second theme I highlighted was *being precise in communicating*, evidenced by #3 (use facts), #6 (choose the right words), and #11 (be aware when you are interpreting).

Respectful Communication

"If we communicated respectfully, what would you see or hear team members say or do...or not say or do?"

Team Note Pad

1. Ask to interrupt.
2. Be on time for meetings.
3. When disagreeing, use facts to challenge or counter argue.
4. Stop talking behind backs
5. Share information; don't withhold
6. Good communication = good tone of voice & body language and choosing the right words.
7. Give constructive feedback, but in private.
8. If we hear/see others in conflict, we'll step in to help, not avoid.
9. Understand each other's roles.
10. Ask for help if needed.
11. Realize when you are assuming or interpreting.
12. For key decisions, use chain of command.

Identify the Most Practical Ideas

Once you notice your themes, there is a tricky but easy-to-master time management challenge.

With eight to 10 behaviors on the flipchart and some general themes highlighted, it is now time to begin identifying the team's most practical ideas. Your goal is to turn these ideas into your proposed intention statement. To do that, you will need to go within to think, which means you will not be actively listening to teammate conversations for a few moments.

So, find a moment when the team is having a good conversation, then mentally disengage from their discussion. Give yourself about 30 seconds to focus on their list of ideas.

My favorite technique to disengage is to pick up a pad of paper and move to the side, a little outside the team's physical space, and begin capturing my potential ideas.

For our example team, I wrote four possible intention statements.

Each teammate will...
1. act in a professional way.
2. communicate in a respectful way with self and customers.
3. resolve conflicts respectfully.
4. give constructive feedback if asked.

After 30 seconds of concentrated analysis, I returned my attention to their conversation and continued listening and capturing more behavior ideas on the public flipchart.

As I recorded, I continued to ask myself,

> *What behavior would most of them agree to keep, and would it provide a context for the other conditions and clarifications?*

I chose to use the second of my four possible intention statements.

Write & Propose an Intention Statement

Intention statements are short, broad, memorable statements that are specific enough to clearly communicate behavioral expectations. You might also think of an intention statement as a category and the conditions for acceptance and clarifications as subcategories.

Just as a team vision statement provides the context for the team's mission, the intention statement provides the overarching behavioral goal for the team's Work Agreement.

Within the context of Right-Minded Teamwork and the Right Choice Model, intention statements describe and define accountable teamwork behavior.

Strong intention statements will represent many of the behaviors listed on your notepad flipchart. Some of the best statements actually use the very words that were captured or circled as evidence of recurring themes.

I highly recommend using the starter phrase *"Each teammate will..."* for most of your Work Agreements simply because it works exceptionally well. It is clear, unambiguous, and most importantly, helps to establish individual interlocking accountability (Step 9).

As the facilitator, you will take responsibility for writing the first suggested intention statement because when you present it to the team, it subconsciously signals the convergence of their conversation. Equally importantly, the team is not yet ready or capable of performing this task.

Do not pull back from the flipchart, turn to the team, and ask,

> *Okay, so what kind of intention statement can we make out of these ideas?*

Up to this point, the team has been mentally and emotionally absorbed in identifying potential solutions. A question like that will be too much of a jolt to their conversational momentum. It is far better for you to suggest an intention statement and facilitate this critical transition, gently leading them from listing behavioral solutions to refining the intention statement.

When you first start facilitating Work Agreements, you may want to come to the workshop prepared with some potential intention statements for the team's desired outcome. However, use your ideas only as a last resort.

It can be scary to be in the middle of a workshop, looking at a flipchart full of ideas, and panicking because you have no clue how to choose the best intention statement. Relax, and trust your intuition as you are analyzing their ideas. In time, your intention-writing skills will improve, and the very best place to practice is in actual Work Agreements workshops. The more you practice, the better you will get at creating statements that you know, even before you propose them, the team will actively embrace.

Here are some excellent, generic intention statement examples:

- Each teammate will resolve or help resolve any / all teamwork issues.

- Each teammate will hold themselves and others accountable for living the letter and spirit of our Vision, Mission, and Values.

- Each leader will do their part to ensure we make good decisions and have an effective decision-making process.

- Each teammate will act and behave in an emotionally mature way.

All of these intention statements are short and clear. To an outsider, they seem elementary. Even though they are easily understood on the surface, they will not mean as much to someone who was not actively engaged in making them.

Good Work Agreements are anything but trite in practice. They are significant and personal for those who create them, even when they seem simple.

The intention statements above came from real teams, and all the people who helped craft them had a visceral and committed connection to them.

Writing an intention statement that creates this kind of loyal connection is your goal.

And here is a tip that I will repeat in Step 8:

As a matter of practice, it is a good idea to write at least one clarification along with your proposed intention statement because it communicates the idea that more clarifications will be written and included in the final Work Agreement.

In just a few pages, you will see an example.

Ah-ha Moments

As you facilitate Agreement workshops, you will soon witness *ah-ha* moments among teammates. These are moments of revelation, clarity, joy, and laughter. They are always associated with a word or a phrase someone said. These moments are a gift to you as a facilitator. Because of their emotional association, they help anchor the team's solidarity and reinforce their commitment to their Work Agreement. For that reason, *you want to use those specific words or phrases* in the team's Work Agreement.

A Reason-able Idea...
Use "ah-ha moment" words.

Here is an example.

An engineering department's desired outcome was to create a culture of individual and team accountability.

After presenting the Right-Minded Choice Model on accountability, I asked the opening question, and ideas started to flow.

Eventually, one very playful engineer said,

> I think if someone keeps acting like a victim, we should send them to the Lower-Loop Lounge.

This, of course, was referencing the Right Choice Model's lower loop of victimization.

When he said it, the team erupted with laughter. So, when it came time to propose the intention statement, I wrote: *"Each teammate will do their part to stay in the upper loop and out of the Lower-Loop Lounge."*

Here's another example with an operations team. Their desired outcome was to address how they would resolve equipment performance issues.

The maintenance manager said,

> My goal for this structure [a deepwater oil production facility] is that when you push the button, the equipment turns on!

To an outsider, this statement may not sound like an ah-ha, but at this particular moment, it was huge. When he said it, the team applauded with joy, laughter, and appreciation.

Rather than asking permission, I went ahead and included that as one of their conditions when I was writing their intention statement. Their condition read, *"Our performance is world-class. We are 100% confident that when we push the button, the equipment turns on."*

Years later, I worked again with both of those teams, and everyone recalled those memorable comments.

Emotions are powerful. Pointing to a joyful or impactful moment within your Agreements' language will help teammates remember and live their Work Agreements in the weeks and months after the workshop.

Now that you've listened, observed, analyzed, identified key ideas, and written your proposed intention statement, it's time to share it with the team.

To present your intention, you say:

> *Okay, you've listed 12 ideas for communicating respectfully, which may go into your Work Agreement. I've written an overarching intention statement and included two possible conditions for acceptance.*
>
> *If you like this intention as it is or with some editing, we can finish your Work Agreement by adding more clarifications or conditions.*
>
> *The intention is ... "Each teammate will communicate in a respectful way with each other and our customers."*

Now, you **stop talking**.

The moment after you propose any intention statement is a transitional moment. It is essential to be quiet. You want to let your proposed statement sink in and be digested.

Most of the time, you will look into their eyes and see a blank stare. Don't fret. They are considering your proposal.

In essence, you are demonstrating respect by giving them time to process what you have proposed. It will only take a few moments before someone responds, and then you can begin facilitating.

Here is what you would have on a new flipchart right next to your notepad flipchart:

Behavioral Agreement – Communication

Intention:

1. Each team member will communicate in a respectful way with each other and our customers.

Clarifications / Conditions for Acceptance:
   A. We will use good communication techniques that include appropriate body language and tone of voice, plus suitable words.
   B. If we see or hear disrespect or we hear an inappropriate behind-back conversation, we own it and need to step in.
   C.

Step 7: Agree on the Intention Statement

After a short dialogue, ask the team if they will live the intention statement.

There are **three guidelines** to remember during this dialogue.

1. You do not want anyone to feel they *have* to accept the intention statement. Ideally, you want teammates to genuinely believe that living this intention will significantly benefit them and their team.

2. Do not work on the conditions list before everyone says yes or at least a conditional yes to an intention statement.

3. It's usually best to write short intention statements because teammates will more likely remember them.

To illustrate these guidelines, we will review two possible scenarios. In the first, everyone agrees to the intention statement with hardly any debate. In the second, there is some disagreement.

A Reason-able Idea…
Typically, the shorter the intention statement is, the more likely teammates will remember it.

Scenario: Everyone Agrees to the Intention Statement

It should take about five minutes to gain everyone's approval for the proposed intention statement. It is typical for teammates to edit your proposed statement, so expect and embrace that. A typical initial response might be:

Well, that makes sense, but it misses several things we listed.

When teammates mention edits or pieces of their list that seem to be missing, you can say:

Yes, you are right, and we'll make a point to work those other things into the conditions and clarifications section. Is that okay?

Stay quiet until someone else responds.

Another person might say something like,

I think your proposed intention summarizes what we have been saying, but I'd like to suggest we put a period after the word 'way' and delete the remaining sentence. I believe we want to be respectful to everyone. Don't we?

That suggestion will generate more discussion. Typical teammate comments might include:

I'm okay with the intention statement. It just seems to be too vague. I have some more clarifications I want to add.

I think we ought to keep it if we all agree to do those other things listed on the other flipchart. I'd also like to scratch out those words and put a period after 'way.'

As you listen to their dialogue, ask yourself if you believe they are telling you and each other the truth. Ask yourself if you believe they will live this Agreement going forward.

If you think they are being honest, look for an opportunity to ask this question:

Okay, as you can see, I've scratched out the last few words after 'way.' If all of you genuinely lived this intention, would it address the respect issue?

Again, be silent after you ask.

If you see or sense they don't believe it will help, you may need to challenge them gently.

If you think their response is sincere enough, and they are just unsure, keep going. When the clarifications and conditions are completed, they will either be committed or not. If they are committed, keep going. If they are not, you will have to facilitate them towards a different intention statement.

If everyone offers a genuine and committed yes to your question above, then say:

> *You have made your first Work Agreement!*
>
> *But you're not done with it yet because we need to capture some of your other ideas and use them as clarifications or conditions for acceptance.*

Pause for a moment and say,

> *You can see that I've already captured some of them on the flipchart. Let me read what I've written to see if you want to keep or edit them, and then I'll ask you another question.*

From there, you move on to Step 8, where you will lead the team through adding clarifications and conditions to their Work Agreement.

Scenario: There Is Some Disagreement with the Intention Statement

Now, let's discuss how to facilitate when there is disagreement over your proposed intention statement.

Even with disagreement, it may only take about five minutes for the team to come to a consensus, but it could also take 10 to 15 minutes.

It is crucial to be accepting if teammates disagree with your proposed intention statement. Just go with their energy.

When this happens, you have two options. The first is to make a simple edit, and the second is to make a significant edit or even create a new intention altogether.

Let's start with the simple edit, which usually happens when someone expresses disagreement by saying,

> *I'm not entirely okay with the statement because it says nothing about our company values. To me, everyone should live by those values, and if they did, we would be respecting one another.*

If you hear a statement like that, you might respond with:

> *Okay, are there particular words you would like to change in the intention statement?*

Many times, a simple edit is all they want. If that is the case, you can either go ahead and change it without asking the team, or you can quickly check-in and ask,

> *What do the rest of you think? Do you want to change it to include company values?*

If there is little resistance, go ahead and try a change. You might say something like,

> *Okay, how about this? Each teammate will live the spirit and letter of our company values.*

Look at the person who suggested it and ask,

> *What do you think about this statement? Shall we use this one instead, and if we did, and the team lived by those values, would that successfully address the respect issue?*

At this point, other teammates will engage in the discussion.

Someone might say,

I favor using the first statement because it will describe respectful behaviors we agree to use, which will align with our company values.

As you facilitate Agreements workshops, you will find most disagreements contain legitimate concerns, even though you may think teammates' ideas are somewhat misplaced.

For instance, a teammate might say,

I'm not disagreeing with the idea of being respectful, but there are times when we have to be brutally honest with one another, with management, and with our customers. I'm concerned that if we accept this statement as it is written, we will not be telling the whole truth.

If you hear a comment like this, there are several good potential responses. As the facilitator, it might be best to step back and let other teammates reply. As you listen to their dialogue, be mindful of what they are saying, and try your best to find appropriate ways to edit the statement, add new conditions, or even write a new intention that addresses legitimate concerns.

If a disagreeing comment suggests a different intention statement altogether, casually move to another blank flipchart and write at the top, *"Each teammate will..."*

Many times, by the time you reach the other flipchart and start the new page, the person will already have given their alternative statement. You can just write it, turn to the team and say,

> *Here is a new intention: Each teammate will respectfully speak their truth.*
>
> *Did I write that correctly? What do others think? Should this be our intention statement?*

They will often come up with a statement that might not be any better than yours or not too different from yours, but if teammates like it, you are still doing your job as their facilitator. If this happens, do not think you have failed them. You have succeeded because they are still very engaged, thanks to your masterful facilitation.

Once everyone agrees to the new intention, ask the closing question:

> *If all of you really and truly lived this new Work Agreement, would it resolve the respect issue?*

By this point, everyone should say yes. You can then move on to Step 8, adding clarifications and conditions.

In most instances, teammates will either agree with your intention statement or disagree slightly and want to create their own. If you have prepared your teammates for the workshop, toxic disagreement will not happen very often. But it occasionally still does. Let's talk about what to do in that scenario.

Rare Scenario: There Is Toxic Disagreement

Although it is infrequent, sometimes a teammate will dramatically disagree with your proposal by saying something similar to:

That isn't even close to what we've been talking about!

Oh my, that is so elementary! I would be embarrassed to tell others we made such a touchy-feely Agreement.

These were actual comments from teammates in two of my workshops.

If someone responds this way, pause, take a deep breath, and say nothing.

Other teammates will often enter the conversation, bringing civility and focus back into the dialogue without your interference. If that doesn't happen, the team leader should step in to manage the situation using the prearranged intervention you jointly created before the workshop.

Please know toxic situations like the above are not typical. Usually, everyone agrees to the intention statement.

Now, as the facilitator, you are ready to move the conversation toward clarifications and conditions for acceptance.

Step 8: Add Clarifications & Conditions for Acceptance

In this step, it is time to incorporate all the other legitimate answers from the notepad flipchart into the team's Work Agreement as clarification or acceptance conditions.

As a matter of practice, it is a good idea to write at least one clarification along with your proposed intention statement because that subconsciously communicates the idea that more clarifications will be written and included in the team's final Work Agreement.

After you have gained additional facilitation experience, you will begin including two or three conditions right away but do not try to write more than four initially. You want the team to engage in transferring them from their notepad flipchart into their budding new Agreement.

It's important for you to mention that although the conditions and clarification are numbered, they are not meant to be in any order of importance or sequence.

You will also want to explain that all of the team's Work Agreements will function in an interrelated manner. It is this interrelated structure, created by the sum of all of their Work Agreements, that makes them such a valuable, worthwhile, powerful, and transformational team-building process.

These Work Agreements describe the team's psychological goal, the second Element of Right-Minded Teamwork's 5 Elements model. They map out how teammates will act and behave while they strive to achieve 100% customer satisfaction.

In other words, a team's set of Work Agreements is, essentially, the **thought system** that describes the team's **Unified Circle of Right-Minded Teamwork Thinking**.

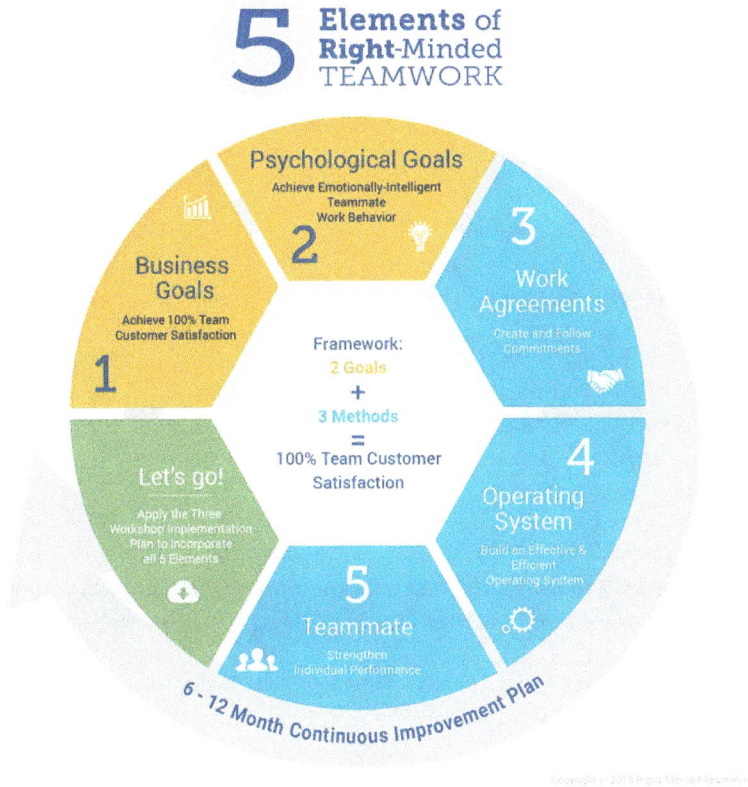

5 **Elements** of **Right**-Minded TEAMWORK

Psychological Goals
Achieve Emotionally-Intelligent Teammate Work Behavior

2

3
Work Agreements
Create and Follow Commitments

Business Goals
Achieve 100% Team Customer Satisfaction

1

Framework:
2 Goals
+
3 Methods
=
100% Team Customer Satisfaction

4
Operating System
Build an Effective & Efficient Operating System

Let's go!
Apply the Three Workshop Implementation Plan to incorporate all 5 Elements

5
Teammate
Strengthen Individual Performance

6 - 12 Month Continuous Improvement Plan

Now let's discuss what you should say and communicate during this step.

In **Step 7**, where the team is discussing and eventually agreeing on their intention statement, you said:

> *You have made your first Work Agreement!*
>
> *But you're not done with it yet because we need to capture some of your other ideas and use them as clarifications or conditions for acceptance.*

Pause for a moment and say,

> *You can see that I've already captured some of them on the flipchart. Let me read what I've written to know if you want to keep or edit them, and then I'll ask you another question.*
>
> *During your discussion over the past half hour, several of you referred to the importance of good communication, so it made sense to summarize your wish by using the three elements that are included in all communication: words, tone, and body language.*
>
> *The first clarification reads, "We will use good communication techniques that include appropriate body language and tone of voice, plus suitable words."*
>
> *What do you think? Do you want to include these as descriptors of being respectful?*

Pause for a moment to see if you are receiving verbal or nonverbal approval.

If teammates agree to this first clarification, draw a line through #6 on the notepad flipchart, then say:

> *The second clarification I've written combines several suggestions that deal with stepping in and helping others who are in conflict, and not withholding. It reads, "If we see or hear disrespect, or we hear inappropriate, behind-the-back conversation, we own it and need to step in."*

Again, pause for a moment to see if they agree with the second condition.

It's not unusual that teammates will like your statement's intent but will want to edit it. If that happens, just review their suggestions, and check with the entire team to see if they agree.

Once you have a consensus, draw a line through #8 on your flipchart.

If you had a list of 12 answers, as we do in our example, it would take the team about 30 to 40 minutes to discuss their solutions and decide whether to include them in the clarifications and conditions.

When the team crosses off all of the answers on the notepad flipchart, turn to the team and ask one or two of the following questions.

Respectful Communication

"If we communicated respectfully, what would you see or hear team members say or do...or not say or do?"

Team Note Pad

1. Ask to interrupt.
2. Be on time for meetings.
3. When disagreeing, use ==facts== to challenge or counter argue.
4. Stop ==talking== behind backs
5. ==Share== information; don't withhold
6. ~~Good communication = good tone of voice & body language and choosing the ==right words==.~~
7. Give constructive feedback, but in private.
8. ~~If we hear/see others in conflict, we'll step in to help, not avoid.~~
9. Understand each other's roles.
10. Ask for help if needed.
11. Realize when you are assuming or ==interpreting==.
12. For key decisions, use chain of command.

Do not ask all of these questions. Don't write them on a flipchart for all to see. Put these questions in your planning notes and ask *just the one or two* that seem the most relevant.

A. *What will prevent you from doing or living this Work Agreement 100% of the time?*

B. *Is this intention practical and doable in your work environment?*

C. *Is there a time, situation, or condition when this intention will not work?*

D. *Is there any situation where you would not feel safe keeping this Work Agreement?*

E. *What internal or external constraints would get in the way of you keeping this Work Agreement?*

F. *Is there anything or anyone that would prevent you from keeping this Work Agreement?*

G. *Is this a clear intention and Work Agreement? Does anything need editing?*

H. *Is everyone clear about what behavior is expected of each teammate?*

Let's say you ask, *"What will prevent you from doing or living this Work Agreement 100% of the time?"*

This is probably my favorite question because it is another reminder of individual choice and accountability. This question usually brings out several more clarifications.

For example, someone might say,

> *I don't think any of us need to remember all the cultural differences of everyone on this team. First of all, I don't know all of them, and second, just because you are of a specific culture does not mean that a particular cultural trait applies to you. I propose that if any teammate believes they've been disrespected, they need to tell the person in private because that person may not even know.*

When you hear a statement like this, go to the flipchart and write:

Condition C: *If someone unintentionally shows disrespect, we will give them the benefit of the doubt, let them know, and create a new way to interact going forward.*

Just as before, turn to the group and ask them if they want to keep this condition.

Let's say you asked this question: *"Is there a time, situation, or condition when this intention would not work?"*

This is an excellent question, too, because it typically brings out legitimate exceptions.

Someone might say,

> *Yes, we have a multicultural team, and there are times when the leader has to make a tough decision. It might feel like disrespect to some, but if she allows everyone to voice their opinions, we all need to actively support her decision even though we might think it is disrespectful.*

Again, you turn to the flipchart and write:

Condition D: *Actively support team decisions in word, deed, and intent.*

Writing clarifications and conditions for acceptance is an essential step because it makes the intention more relevant. It clarifies the intention and can eliminate any ambiguity about how teammates have agreed to behave going forward.

Remember, a team's first Work Agreement will take longer to complete than subsequent Agreements. Typically, for a group of 15 people, it could take an hour or more to go through all 10.

If an hour has gone by, and you believe the team could talk for another thirty minutes, you may have a team that is making this effort too complicated. That means they are likely creating too many conditions and overly long clarifications.

There is no perfect number for how many conditions a team needs for their first Work Agreement, but you might have as many as ten.

When the team has listed five or six conditions, begin asking closing questions like,

> *What do you think? Is this Work Agreement complete enough?*
>
> *Do you believe everyone understands what we're all agreeing to do?*

If they want to list more conditions and it makes sense to you, go with their inclinations.

If they seem to be getting too complex, you may have to say something like,

> *Before we discuss another condition, I want to advocate for the concept that your Work Agreements do not need to be complicated.*
>
> *They should be relatively short but clear and straightforward. That way, they will be easier to remember.*
>
> *Said another way, Work Agreements work well when you commit to living the spirit and intent rather than trying to remember all the specifics.*

Nevertheless, you want to go through the entire list of legitimate answers captured on your notepad flipchart and decide to either include them or not. As you discuss each item in the list, draw a line through it to demonstrate everyone's voice was heard and incorporated into the Work Agreement.

Respectful Communication

"If we communicated respectfully, what would you see or hear team members say or do...or not *say or do?"*

Team Note Pad

1. ~~Ask to interrupt.~~
2. ~~Be on time for meetings.~~
3. ~~When disagreeing, use facts to challenge or counter argue.~~
4. ~~Stop talking behind backs~~
5. ~~Share information; don't withhold~~
6. ~~Good communication = good tone of voice & body language and choosing the right words.~~
7. ~~Give constructive feedback, but in private.~~
8. ~~If we hear/see others in conflict, we'll step in to help, not avoid.~~
9. ~~Understand each other's roles.~~
10. ~~Ask for help if needed.~~
11. ~~Realize when you are assuming or interpreting.~~
12. ~~For key decisions, use chain of command.~~

Once everything is crossed off, your Agreement will look like this:

Behavioral Agreement – Communication

Team Choice: Intention Statement
1. Each teammate will communicate in a respectful way.

Clarifications / Conditions for Acceptance:

A. We will use good communication techniques that include appropriate body language and tone of voice, plus suitable words.
B. If we see or hear disrespect or we hear inappropriate behind back conversation, we own it and need to step in.
C. If someone unintentionally shows disrespect we will give them the benefit of the doubt, let them know and create a new way to interact going forward.
D. We will actively support team decisions in word, deed and energy; for key decisions we will use our decision-making protocol agreement.
E. We will be on time to meetings.
F. We will ask, "May I interrupt you?"
G. We will use observable facts during disagreements and decision-making and we will acknowledge when we are using assumptions.
H. We will understand each other's roles, ask for help if we need it, share relevant information and if helpful, give constructive feedback in private.
I.

Now that everyone believes they have the right conditions and clarifications for their Work Agreement, you have a choice to make.

You either move the conversation towards creating an interlocking accountability condition, described in Step 9, or you move to Step 10, the final step, which is about declaring commitment.

As stated before, there is no one right way to facilitate Work Agreements.

However, creating an interlocking accountability condition is an especially good idea at the end of a team's first Work Agreement. It will set the tone going forward and will apply to all team Agreements, meaning you only have to create this condition once.

Step 9: Create Interlocking Accountability

Create an interlocking accountability condition statement by finishing the sentence,

"If someone continues to break this Work Agreement, we will..."

Interlocking accountability means:

- Giving positive reinforcement when someone continues to do a great job of living their Work Agreements.

- Confronting someone in a supportive and safe but firm way if they continue to break the spirit or letter of the team's Work Agreement.

- Being accountable to each other for achieving or accomplishing the desired outcome of the Work Agreements.

- Strengthening team spirit and trust by recovering and learning from mistakes rather than denying or punishing those who make mistakes.

- Creating and sustaining teammate trust because teammates who believe everyone will live their part of the Work Agreement ultimately create Right-Minded Teamwork.

Interlocking accountability is crucial to the success of a team's Work Agreements. It is prudent to include a statement that defines interlocking responsibility in at least one of the team's Work Agreements, ideally the first one. This condition should then also apply to all additional team Agreements.

Two Guidelines

There are **two essential guidelines** for creating interlocking accountability:

1. Don't skip this step.

2. Introduce the concept of interlocking accountability at *the right time* and in *the right way.*

Inevitably, some teammates will break their Work Agreements very soon after the workshop.

Typically, these are unconscious mistakes, but they will happen. That is why it is practical to have an interlocking accountability condition, especially for those who continue to break the Agreements.

Teams that have defined their interlocking accountability method increase their likelihood of recovering from difficult situations. Teams that do *not* have this condition do not recover as fast. Some teams never recover at all. When that happens, the Work Agreement process is often unjustly labeled a failure.

For this reason, it is vitally important for teammates to understand they must actively live their Work Agreements after the workshop for them to benefit the team and the team's customers.

A saying from *A Course in Miracles* describes it perfectly: *"To say these words means nothing; to live these words means everything."*

Creating Work Agreements is the equivalent of "saying these words." But the payoff comes from "living these words" after the workshop ends.

In other words,

Work Agreements mean everything when teammates live them.

For most teams, having a condition that addresses how to supportively confront a teammate who continually breaks a team Agreement is exceedingly prudent. But even when teammates recognize this truth, many teammates will still break the Agreements. Be upfront with your team about the likelihood of broken Agreements. Share with them that it is normal developmental behavior.

At the same time, remind them broken Agreements are not a reason to abandon their Agreements altogether. Instead, they will want and need to recover and learn from the break. Tell them they may need to edit their Agreement slightly, but no matter what, teammates need to recommit, heal, and move on.

Teammates need to believe in the strength of their commitments and maintain their convictions to live their Agreements. Remind them that, in time, the behaviors outlined in their Agreements will become second nature. They will use them consistently, without having to think about it.

When they achieve that level of fidelity with their Agreements, they will rarely need to use their interlocking agreements to correct behavior.

As for introducing interlocking accountability at the right time and in the right way, I encourage you to trust your intuition as to when and how to do it. With most teams, you will not meet resistance. However, you can *create* resistance if you go overboard in advocating for including this condition.

Typically, you want to introduce this concept during the team's first Work Agreements workshop. The best time to introduce it is after Step 8. Let's discuss how you would do that.

Imagine you are at the point in the dialogue where the team has created eight to 10 condition statements. It's been a good discussion, and you believe the Work Agreement they are about to consummate will indeed help them achieve their desired outcome.

It would seem natural to ask everyone if they would commit to living the Work Agreement, which is Step 10. But before you do that, consider introducing interlocking accountability.

If it is the right time, here is how you could present it to the team using our example of communicating respectfully:

Let me share something that might be a little difficult to accept, but give me a moment to hear me out, okay?

It is likely that many, if not all of you, will unintentionally break this Work Agreement.

I'm saying this because we have all made personal resolutions to change something about ourselves, only to realize that we didn't keep them.

This does not make us inadequate or incompetent. We might just have forgotten, or we might be struggling to change old habits.

So, if someone breaks our Work Agreements, it might be unintentional. Don't we want to remind them and support them? And don't you want to be told in a supportive way?

Furthermore, if someone continues to break the Agreement, even after a few supportive reminders, it is far better to have an agreed-upon method as to how you want to address that situation.

It's wiser to have this condition and not use it than to face a tough situation and try to address it without an interlocking accountability agreement.

Then, you pause.

Typically, at this stage, several people will chime in to say it would be valuable to have this condition. Their comments will also give you ideas to determine the right words to use and the appropriate level of complexity for the condition.

After you present the concept of interlocking accountability, go to the flipchart, and write a new condition:

Behavioral Agreement – Communication

Team Choice: Intention Statement
   1. Each teammate will communicate in a respectful way.

Clarifications / Conditions for Acceptance:

   A. We will use good communication techniques that include appropriate body language and tone of voice, plus suitable words.
   B. If we see or hear disrespect or we hear an inappropriate behind-the-back conversation, we own it and need to step in.
   C. If someone unintentionally shows disrespect, we will give them the benefit of the doubt, let them know, and create a new way to interact going forward.
   D. We will actively support team decisions in word, deed, and energy; we will use our decision-making protocol agreement for key decisions.
   E. We will be on time for meetings.
   F. We will ask, "May I interrupt you?"
   G. We will use observable facts during disagreements and decision-making, and we will acknowledge when we are using assumptions.
   H. We will understand each other's roles, ask for help if we need it, share relevant information and if helpful, give constructive feedback in private.
   I. If someone continues to break this agreement,

Then turn to the group and say:

> *Let's complete this sentence: "If someone continues to break this Agreement, we will..."*

If your team's dialogue has gone well up to this point, someone will usually say something playful, like:

> *Fire them!*

A light-hearted comment will produce some laughter and smiles, which is good pressure relief.

At that moment, you must decide whether the team needs only a simple condition that will take about one or two minutes to complete or whether they need a more complicated condition.

Usually, you'll just need to repeat the question:

> *If someone continues to break this Work Agreement, assuming the first break was unintentional, what do you suggest?*
>
> *What would you like someone to do or say to you if they thought you were continuing to break this Agreement?*

Someone might make a legitimate and straightforward statement such as:

> *I would want them to approach me and tell me their truth. If I disagree with them, I will suggest we ask a third party, a neutral teammate, to join us and help us find a solution.*

For many teams, this is perfect and reasonably sufficient. Without saying a word, you can go to the flipchart and write:

> *If someone continues to break this Agreement, we will tell them and invite a third party to help if the disagreement continues.*

Then you could ask:

> *What do you think? Is this practical, and is it sufficient for our team?*

If everyone says yes, it's time to move on to closure and commitment in Step 10.

Please note this entire interlocking accountability discussion might last only two or three minutes. It does not have to be a long conversation.

But if you, or others, believe this condition needs more detail, the discussion could lead to an additional, more complex condition, such as:

> *If someone continues to break this Agreement, we will tell them, and if the disagreement continues, we will invite a third party to help. If that doesn't solve the issue, we will all go to a higher authority for support and resolution.*

It is not absolutely necessary to create an interlocking accountability condition, and you do not have to complete it for the first Agreement. However, most teams are glad they have this agreed-upon method in place, just in case. It also helps, in a subliminal way, to proactively stop repeat offenders because they know they will be confronted.

Remember, you only need to create this condition for one Work Agreement because it should also apply to all subsequent Agreements.

Now, it's time for the last step: to ask everyone to commit to the Agreement.

Behavioral Agreement – Communication

Team Choice: Intention Statement
1. Each teammate will communicate in a respectful way.

Clarifications / Conditions for Acceptance:

A. We will use good communication techniques that include appropriate body language and tone of voice, plus suitable words.
B. If we see or hear disrespect or we hear an inappropriate behind-the-back conversation, we own it and need to step in.
C. If someone unintentionally shows disrespect, we will give them the benefit of the doubt, let them know, and create a new way to interact going forward.
D. We will actively support team decisions in word, deed, and energy; we will use our decision-making protocol agreement for key decisions.
E. We will be on time for meetings.
F. We will ask, "May I interrupt you?"
G. We will use observable facts during disagreements and decision-making, and we will acknowledge when we are using assumptions.
H. We will understand each other's roles, ask for help if we need it, share relevant information and if helpful, give constructive feedback in private.
I. If someone continues to break this agreement, we will tell them that we will invite a third party to help if there is continued disagreement. If that doesn't solve the issues, we will all go to a higher authority for support and resolution.

Step 10: Final Work Agreement

Creating a Work Agreement takes energy, but living the Agreement will achieve the team's desired outcome. Therefore, it's vital for each teammate to publicly declare they commit to living the Work Agreement going forward.

Your final task is to gain approval, and, when everyone approves, conduct a short celebration before moving on to the second teamwork topic.

Therefore, it's vital for each teammate to publicly declare they commit to living the Work Agreement going forward. Set it up so that each person, in a sincere way, states their commitment with appropriate enthusiasm.

Here's one way to set it up:

> *Congratulations! You have created a terrific Work Agreement. Will this Agreement ensure that you achieve your outcome?*

Everyone will say yes, and then you say:

> *I'm going to go around the room and ask each of you a question. If you agree, then say yes with enthusiasm to show you mean it.*
>
> *Do you agree to hold yourself accountable for living this Agreement, and will you hold others responsible, in a supportive way, for living this Agreement?*

Walk towards the first person, and they will usually say yes. Then gently point to the next person and wait for them to say yes. Go around the room until everyone has said yes.

Don't let your guard down. As you go from person to person, you may find someone who does not yet believe in the Agreement. If you facilitate this step in an affirming and caring way, you will respectfully bring out those nonbelievers.

How will you know who they are? When you point to them, and it is their turn to say yes, they will say "no" outright, or they will squirm.

If they say no, then you have a potential problem.

Gently ask:

> *Is there a particular part of the Agreement you would like to change?*

If they say yes, and they explain that they are bothered by a particular word or phrase, ask:

> *What word can we use that would be better for you?*

Whatever word they choose, if it is a legitimate behavior, write it on the flipchart and ask the team if it is okay.

Most of the time, the team will agree. Then go back to the person and ask them to commit. Most of the time, they'll say yes.

If a teammate says that they "just don't like" the entire Agreement or one particular part, then you know they have withheld their thoughts and feelings throughout the whole conversation. They've been dishonest with their teammates.

This situation rarely happens, but when it does, it has the potential to derail the conversation. Sometimes it will cause an argument.

If it does, stay calm and first let fellow teammates confront the person in a supportive way. They will still need to interact with this teammate going forward. This situation allows them the perfect opportunity to practice their Work Agreement with your facilitation help.

The goal is to ask this resisting person to communicate, in behavioral terms, what they want to include or exclude in the Agreement. Try offering specific suggestions; the Agreement may only need a little more help.

It is possible that you and the team leader anticipated this reaction and had prepared an intervention ahead of time to address this situation.

For example, during pre-workshop interviews, I recommended that you and the team leader communicate that, in the workshop, the team would be making collective Work Agreements and that all teammates would actively participate in creating those Agreements.

During those pre-workshop interviews, you will have shared that if the team could not reach a consensus on a particular Agreement, the fallback would be that the team leader would make the final decision.

So, the worst thing that can happen is the person who is resisting says they just don't want the Agreement and refuses to offer specific suggestions, in which case the leader may need to make the final call.

This level of resistance is not common. In my facilitating career of over three decades, this situation happened only twice. If it happens, take a break, and confer directly with the team leader and the individual. Typically, this will overcome the problem.

The vast majority of the time, finalizing the Work Agreement takes only two to four minutes. It typically feels exceptionally good to all and provides a sense of relief.

You may find many people thinking, feeling, and even saying things like,

> *We now have a real-world, practical Agreement. This is extremely exciting!*

At this point in the workshop, it is time for the team to take a break and then come back to address the second outcome on the agenda.

Your transition comment could be:

> *Again, congratulations! This Agreement successfully addresses today's first outcome: respect (point to the agenda on the wall).*
>
> *After a 15-minute break, we will come back and address the second outcome, which is to create a decision-making protocol Agreement.*

During the break, post the final Agreement flipcharts on the meeting room wall.

While you are doing this, don't be surprised if teammates express their positive opinions and gratitude for your guidance and support.

Behavioral Agreement – Communication

Team Choice: Intention Statement
1. Each teammate will communicate in a respectful way.

Clarifications / Conditions for Acceptance:

A. We will use good communication techniques that include appropriate body language and tone of voice, plus suitable words.
B. If we see or hear disrespect or we hear an inappropriate behind-the-back conversation, we own it and need to step in.
C. If someone unintentionally shows disrespect, we will give them the benefit of the doubt, let them know, and create a new way to interact going forward.
D. We will actively support team decisions in word, deed, and energy; we will use our decision-making protocol agreement for key decisions.
E. We will be on time for meetings.
F. We will ask, "May I interrupt you?"
G. We will use observable facts during disagreements and decision-making, and we will acknowledge when we are using assumptions.
H. We will understand each other's roles, ask for help if we need it, share relevant information and if helpful, give constructive feedback in private.
I. If someone continues to break this agreement, we will tell them that we will invite a third party to help if there is continued disagreement. If that doesn't solve the issues, we will all go to a higher authority for support and resolution.

Signing Agreements

Every so often, a teammate will suggest that all teammates sign their Work Agreements.

In my experience, this is not necessary, so I do not include it in the instructions. However, if most or all teammates want to sign their Agreement, go for it.

Here is just one example.

This particular team created six Agreements in their first workshop.

Instead of signing all six, I took a flipchart and wrote at the top an intention statement to "live the spirit and intent" of the collective Agreements.

Everyone signed underneath, and they posted the flipchart in their team meeting room.

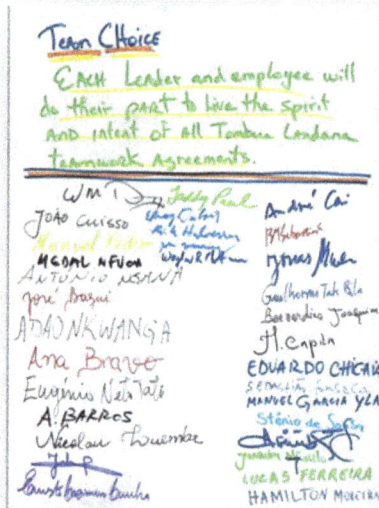

Work Agreements:
How to Sustain Them

How do teammates successfully live and sustain their new Work Agreements?

They periodically review and modify them.

Below are specific ideas on how to do just that, followed by a checklist of Work Agreement questions to help you ensure you've created solid, realistic Agreements that will work for your team. After that, you'll find a real-world story about a team's journey to creating their Work Agreements, including a true "moment of Reason."

Ideas for Sustainable Agreements

1. A week after creating the Agreements, the entire team spends 15 to 30 minutes reviewing their Agreements to:

   a. be certain all teammates understand the desired agreed-upon behaviors
   b. modify Agreements if necessary
   c. recommit to living the Agreements going forward

2. The team also conducts a more thorough review of their Agreements every 90 days.

    a. If your team uses RMT's 90-Day Team Operating System, you are applying the *Team Performance Factor Assessment.* Performance Factor #25 asked how well your teammates are living your Work Agreements.

    b. It's not unusual for teams to keep their Work Agreements for a year or more. However, when all teammates truly live them, in time, it's okay to delete an Agreement or meld part of one Agreement into another.

    c. Said another way, Work Agreements are evergreen. They can live on, be modified, or even be happily released once they have achieved their outcome.

3. Use the *Work Agreement Checklist* below in your reviews.

4. Between reviews, teammates are encouraged to acknowledge other teammates for keeping the Agreements.

    a. This is practical positive reinforcement, a win-win for everyone. It's an emotionally mature, Right-Minded way to treat each other.

5. If your team conducts regular meetings, consider holding a one-minute "Agreement review" of one Agreement at the beginning of each session.

    a. You can do this for a month or two until the Agreements are well understood and followed. This is another opportunity to give positive reinforcement to specific teammates.

6. Consider posting your Work Agreements in your team meeting room or in a visible place where the Agreements can be easily and frequently seen. Here is a photograph of one team's three Work Agreements.

   a. Consider asking teammates to include their Work Agreements in their performance reviews.

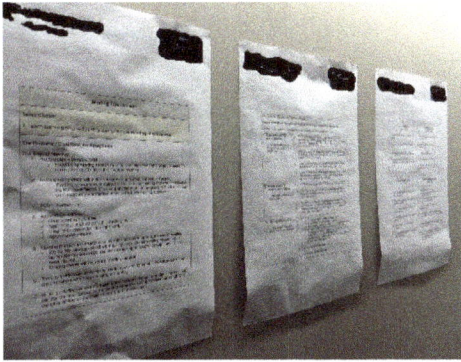

Work Agreement Checklist

Do our Work Agreements…

1. Guide our team on how to increase trust or how to earn it back if it's lost?

2. Address how teammates intend to acknowledge themselves and others for a job well done?

3. Tell us how we're doing in terms of holding ourselves and others accountable in a safe and supportive way?

4. Address how we will get back on track if a teammate is avoiding an interpersonal or business conflict?

5. Guide us in how to deal with a teammate when / if they triangulate others into a tense situation or conflict?

6. Provide us with a clear and agreed-upon process for resolving misunderstandings or conflicts?

7. Give us guidance on how to dialogue about delicate interpersonal styles?

8. Address how we will clear up confusion or disagreements in how decisions are made?

9. Declare that all teammates will hold themselves and others accountable when / if someone slips and does not honor the letter and the spirit of the team's Work Agreements (when / if they break the interlocking accountability condition)?

"We've Already Agreed How
We Were to Address that Issue, Haven't We?"

One year after their first Work Agreements workshop, this team had completely turned around.

In just a year, they experienced:

- ✓ 78% increase in teammate **trust**
- ✓ 46% increase in **mutual team member support**
- ✓ 61% increase in **complying with decisions**
- ✓ Over **$350,000 in savings**

This was a Field Operations team for a major oil company in the Gulf of Mexico. They were responsible for supporting all the company's offshore oil platforms.

Before I met them, they were competent, but they were unhappy and far from productive. Worst of all, two-thirds of the team members were arrogant and aggressive.

They turned to me for facilitative support.

How & Why They Created Their Agreements

In their first team-building workshop, the team created two Work Agreements.

Three months later, those Agreements led to a **"Moment of Reason."**

I will explain what that means, but first, let me share their story chronologically.

Before any team-building workshop, as the facilitator, I first diagnose the team's current performance level. That means using one or two methods:

1. Administering a Team Perception Survey
2. Interviewing teammates

With this team, I chose to do both.

First, I conducted a Team Perception Survey so I could understand how they assessed their current performance.

Teammate **trust**, one of the 20 performance factors measured in the survey, came in low, just 3.13 out of a possible 7.00. From that measure, I knew things were pretty bad. We had our work cut out for us.

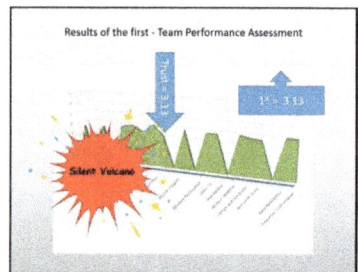

Results of the first - Team Performance Assessment

After studying the survey results, I then interviewed all nine teammates individually. During the interviews, I learned about several teamwork dysfunctions. A number of teammates commented about the tendency of several other teammates to "explode" when they became frustrated.

I called that behavior **Silent Volcano Dysfunction**.

In the first workshop, I presented a Silent Volcano graphic illustration of their behavior to clarify the pattern.

Please take a moment and read it now. I bet you have seen this pattern before, too.

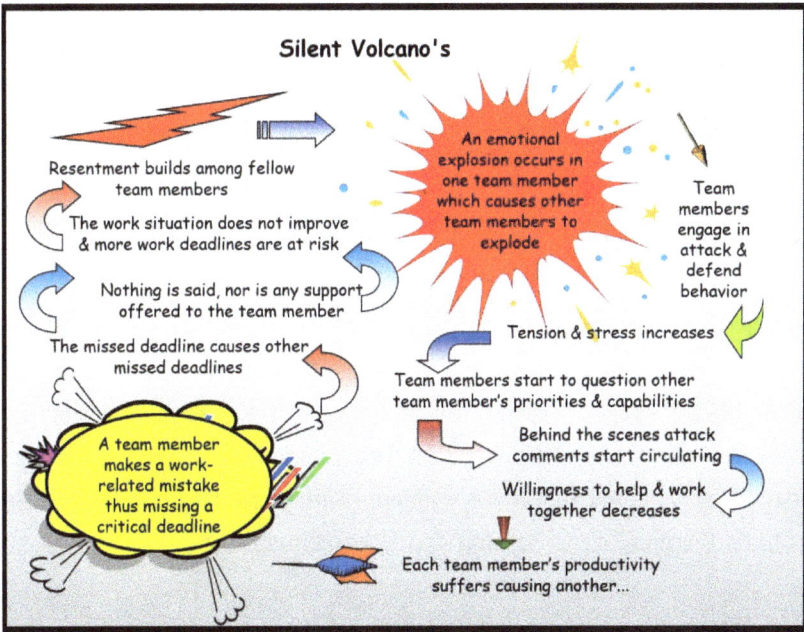

When the team saw this graphic, they knew it described their behavior. They realized and accepted that they, as a team, had to change.

Moreover, they were willing to address their differences to make it happen.

Consequently, they chose two topics for their first Work Agreements:

1. Lack of **trust**
2. How to become a successful, **self-managing team**

After they chose their first two topics, I presented the **Right-Minded Choice Model.**

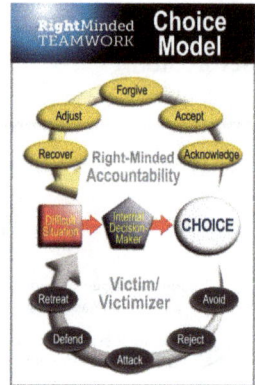

The Model teaches that we only have two choices for responding to difficult situations: in an accountable way or as a victim.

The team liked the Right Choice Model. They believed it would help them resolve their two issues.

After a short discussion, they agreed to act and behave in an accountable way. Moreover, they actually agreed on specific behaviors from the Right-Minded Teamwork Attitudes & Behaviors list. Their selected teamwork behaviors played an important role in helping them create three team Work Agreements.

All three Work Agreements were behavioral Agreements that addressed how they would increase trust. The other three Agreements helped them become a self-managing team, which was a new requirement from their senior leaders.

The team agreed to conduct follow-up team-building workshops once every three months. They asked me to facilitate these workshops and to administer a new survey each time. I worked with them for two years.

Three months after the first workshop, I administered the second survey. The results already showed improvement. Teammate trust had increased from 3.13 to 3.90 - a decent-sized jump for just three months.

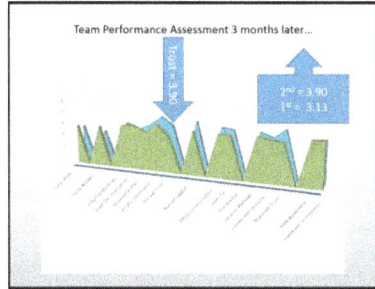

Seeing their growth made teammates even more motivated to continue teamwork improvement.

A Breakthrough "Moment of Reason" at the Three-Month Mark

In the second workshop, the team experienced a pivotal moment of accord around their Agreements. This collective teammate moment was a **"moment of Reason."**

*A **moment of Reason** is a shift in one's mind. It is a moment when sanity and good behavior return to the minds of those who have been temporarily out of their Right Minds.*

Their Moment of Reason changed the way these nine teammates treated and worked with each other.

What Happened?

About an hour into the workshop, the team fell back into their old way of interacting. They were once again arguing about something they had addressed three months earlier.

At one point, I was able to interrupt their bickering. I asked them to pull out their team Work Agreements. They all read them. Then, one teammate said,

> *We've already agreed how we were to address that issue, haven't we?*

I replied,

> *Yes. Now, **you only have two choices - be a victim or be accountable**. You can argue and fight more, or you can recommit to your Work Agreements.*

In less than a minute, they agreed to recommit to their Work Agreements.

It was their **moment of Reason**.

It was a perfect example of how teammates, who are out of their minds, can move back into their right minds.

They made this shift quickly and easily by **remembering *their* team Work Agreements.**

For the rest of the second workshop, the third workshop, and beyond, they never slipped back to their old ways. As the third and fourth surveys showed, the team continued to improve over the next six months.

Results:
One Year of Following Their Agreements

A year after establishing their Work Agreements, the team presented the following results to their Senior Leadership Team.

- ✓ 78% increase in teammate **trust**
- ✓ 46% increase in **mutual team member support**
- ✓ 61% increase in **complying with decisions**
- ✓ Over **$350,000 in savings**

Finally, the teammates were happy and productive. Furthermore, their leaders and the team's customers were also happy.

The team continued to improve and work together for another five years. They never returned to their old, dysfunctional ways.

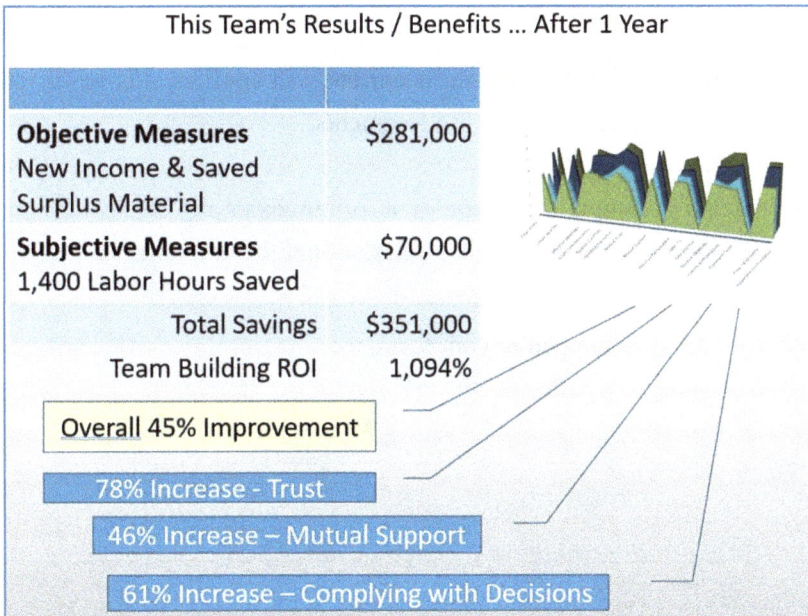

This Team's Results / Benefits ... After 1 Year

Objective Measures New Income & Saved Surplus Material	$281,000
Subjective Measures 1,400 Labor Hours Saved	$70,000
Total Savings	$351,000
Team Building ROI	1,094%

Overall 45% Improvement

78% Increase - Trust

46% Increase – Mutual Support

61% Increase – Complying with Decisions

Why Team Agreements Work

In my 35-year career, facilitated over 500 teams in seven countries in my 35-year team-building career. I worked with many of those teams for several years. Every team created some kind of team Work Agreement, and every team grew and succeeded because of it.

Work Agreements work when teammates live and follow them.

Here's why:

It is not a matter of *if* conflict will happen, but *when* conflict happens among teammates.

This truth alone is enough justification for creating team Work Agreements.

It is far better to have Work Agreements in place before conflict happens. But even if your team is currently in conflict, it is never too late to create and follow Work Agreements.

This team's compelling story is a prime example of how Work Agreements help teams. But it is certainly not the only one.

This success can happen in your team, too.

The End.
Your New Beginning.

When all 5 Elements of Right-Minded Teamwork's core framework are fully released into your team's operating system, **including Work Agreements**, you have established the proper conditions for successfully achieving Right-Minded Teamwork.

Imagine…

You are now thinking and behaving in a Right-Minded way. You are self-aware and focused on achieving your **team's business** and **psychological goals**. You consistently strive for **100% customer satisfaction**, and you always aim to **do no harm** while **working as one**.

To guide your steps, you have purposeful team **Work Agreements** describing your team's thought system. You get work done by leveraging your **Team Operating System**, identifying the critical few, focusing on solutions, and making true improvements.

As Right-Minded Teammates, you **willfully follow Reason**, behaving mindfully and positively navigating difficult team situations. You have risen far above Ego's battleground to joyfully engage with one another in your work classroom, learning and growing every day. Happily, you find yourselves living more and more often in the **Unified Circle of Right-Minded Teamwork Thinking**.

Your New Beginning

Now that you understand each of Right-Minded Teamwork's 5 Elements and how they will benefit your team, you are ready to implement RMT in your team. Remember, even though there is no single right way to implement RMT, the three-workshop Implementation Plan presented earlier in these pages will always work.

So, gather your teammates, and conduct your first workshop. Live your new team Work Agreements for a month or two, and then conduct the second workshop. Trust the process. Keep moving forward.

When you finish the third teammate development workshop, your team will begin following your customized 90-day team operating plan. Every quarter, you will get to measure your progress and success. Each time, you will reinforce the value of RMT in your team.

Don't Forget!

As you begin your journey to Right-Minded Teamwork, don't forget: good teamwork does not just happen on its own. It must be cultivated, tended, and encouraged.

To bring your team together, you need guidance from proven, real-world methods, such as Right-Minded Teamwork. Moreover, you and your teammates must sincerely want to receive and follow this guidance, or the powerful teachings will be meaningless. Good teamwork must be a collaborative venture of commitment and growth.

If you want better teamwork, Right-Minded Teamwork can show you how to get there and what to do, but only with your help. Together with your teammates, you must believe that you have what it takes. With that conviction and Reason's guidance, you will collectively create and sustain Right-Minded Teamwork.

Now, go and create Right-Minded Teamwork for yourself and your team, and know that *you are making the world better for everyone, everywhere, forever*.

The End

Thanks for reading our Right-Minded Teamwork book. If you enjoyed it, please take a moment to leave a review at your favorite retailer or RightMindedTeamwork.com.

For a deeper understanding of RMT concepts and terms, flip forward a few more pages to find an in-depth *Glossary of Right-Minded Teamwork Terms and Resources.*

On behalf of Reason and all the Right-Minded Teammate Decision-Makers of the world, best wishes to you and your teammates as you create your own *Right-Minded Team that Works Together as One*.

DECISION MAKER

REASON

About the Author

The idea of "developing people and teams that work" began as a company statement for organizational consulting firm Lord & Hogan LLC, founded in 1990. Leveraging his personable but results-oriented consulting style, founder **Dan Hogan** devoted his career to transforming dysfunctional work relationships into positive, supportive bonds.

But over the course of his 40-year career, something shifted.

Through his work as an organizational development coach, performance consultant, and Certified Master Facilitator, the mission of Lord & Hogan also became Dan's own.

Better Work Relationships = Stronger, More Productive Teams

As a consultant and facilitator, Dan advocated for the individuals and managed teams he served. He emphasized the equal importance of strong team member relationships and solid business systems and processes to overall business success. His efforts spoke for themselves as his clients began to notice results.

With Dan's guidance, teams were more productive almost overnight. There were fewer day-to-day interpersonal issues. Project management efforts were finally back on track. Teams were achieving their goals.

After being stuck for so long, these teams were moving forward... smoothly. As one client said, "Dan has the unique ability to hear the confusion and bring clarity. He has helped me, our team, and our organization to move to the next level."

The Right-Minded Teamwork Model: A Legacy

Not only did Dan's efforts deliver consistent, powerful results (gaining him many long-term clients over the years) at a higher level, but his work also positively impacted the practice of behavioral change management.

Over the course of his career, Dan refined his ideas along with the help of his clients and the teams he served. Eventually, he created his own proprietary tools, processes, and strategies. Of all his models and creations, Dan's most significant accomplishment has been the development of his Right-Minded Teamwork model, which perfectly assembles all his tools and processes into a single, streamlined approach.

At its core, Right-Minded Teamwork (RMT) is a continuous improvement loop for small and large groups; it has been proven to work with teams of all sizes. No matter what team challenges or interpersonal issues are happening, RMT has the power to correct them.

By first bringing the team together under a unified set of goals, then providing tools for teams to explore, understand, and work through their underlying concerns, Right-Minded Teamwork provides teams with the opportunity to address unproductive behaviors in a safe, non-condemning way. Focusing on acceptance, forgiveness, and self-adjustment among teammates, Right-Minded Teamwork directly addresses and resolves the root cause of even the most difficult teamwork situations.

After directly serving over 500 teams in seven countries and creating lasting tools and resources that will go on to support countless additional teams, leaders, and facilitators on every continent, Dan Hogan has left a legacy to be proud of. No longer an active facilitator, Dan has transformed his ideas and contributions into powerful, effective, team-building tools available online, providing team facilitators and team leaders around the globe access to Right-Minded Teamwork.

Books by Dan Hogan

Reason, Ego & the Right-Minded Teamwork Myth: *The Philosophy and Process for Creating a Right-Minded Team That Works Together as One*

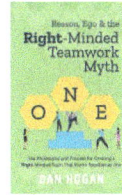

This book explores two foundational concepts: the Right-Minded Teamwork Myth, a short tale that presents RMT's underlying teamwork philosophy, and the Right-Minded Teamwork team-building process, a step-by-step approach to implementing RMT in any team.

Right-Minded Teamwork in Any Team: *The Ultimate Team-Building Method to Create a Team That Works as One*

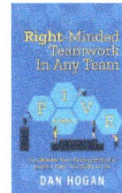

Right-Minded Teamwork is built on a framework of 5 Elements, explored in this book. These two goals and three methods are implemented into your team through three team-building workshops conducted over a six-to-12-month period. Once your team completes its third workshop, you move into a 90-day, continuous improvement operating plan that allows your team to achieve their goals, do no harm, and work together as one.

How to Facilitate Team Work Agreements*: A Practical, 10-Step Process for Building a Right-Minded Team That Works as One*

Team Work Agreements are collective pledges made by your team to transform non-productive or dysfunctional actions into positive and constructive work behavior. Though this book is written primarily for team facilitators, team leaders, and teammates may also follow these steps to create powerful, effective Work Agreements to solve and prevent interpersonal and process problems.

How to Apply the Right Choice Model*: Create a Right-Minded Team That Works as One*

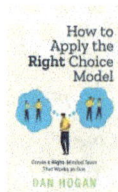

The concept of Right Choice states every person has free will. Free will means you are 100% responsible for how you respond to every situation, circumstance, and event. When difficult team problems occur, you either act as an ally or an adversary. When you choose to be an ally, you demonstrate positive, accountable behavior. When you are an adversary, you behave as either a victim or a victimizer. This book and model will guide you through creating a team of productive, supportive, Right-Minded teammate allies.

7 Mindfulness Training Lessons: Improve Teammates' Ability to Work as One with Right-Minded Thinking

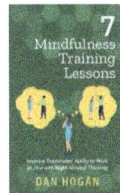

If you want your team to work together as one, you want them to think as one, too. These 7 Mindfulness Training Lessons will help you achieve a positive team mindset by guiding teammates to raise their awareness of thoughts, choices, and behaviors. Teammates may also use these lessons to create the team's Right-Minded thought system. The 7 Lessons can be summed up in one sentence, emphasizing three words: Right-Minded Teammates **accept**, **forgive**, and **adjust** their thinking and work behavior. When teammates follow these lessons, they **do no harm** while **working together as one.**

Right-Minded Teamwork: 9 Right Choices for Building a Team That Works as One

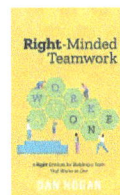

This quick read is an excellent Right-Minded Teamwork primer and a terrific way to introduce RMT to teammates. These nine teamwork choices are universal, self-evident, and self-validating. You want them in your team. In this book, each of the 9 Right Choices is defined, and exercises are provided for applying each choice.

Design a Right-Minded, Team-Building Workshop: *12 Steps to Create a Team That Works as One*

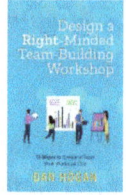

This book includes complete instructions on how to design a practical, real-world, team-building workshop that teammates actually want to attend. Unlike many team activities labeled "team building" that are really more "team bonding," true team-building workshops are intentionally designed to solve a team's real-world problems. Written primarily for team facilitators, team leaders, and teammates may also follow these 12 steps to design an effective, transformative team workshop.

Achieve Your Organization's Strategic Plan: *Create a Right-Minded Team Management System to Ensure All Teams Work as One*

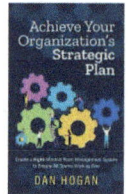

When a single team within an organization works together as one, they are effective and productive. When an enterprise works with the same level of synergy, it is exponentially more powerful. A Team Management System, like the Right-Minded Teamwork TMS model taught in this book, lays the groundwork for your organization to get every team on the same page. By following RMT's four-part rollout plan, create and deploy your own Team Management System, align teammate attitudes and work behavior with company values, and bring your entire organization together to work as one and achieve your strategic plan.

Glossary of Right-Minded Teamwork Terms & Resources

100% Customer Satisfaction

Creating 100% customer satisfaction is a primary goal of Right-Minded Teamwork. Your team is responsible for providing quality products and services to customers; for your team and enterprise to succeed, your customers deserve to be 100% satisfied.

With a strong customer satisfaction plan, as described in *Right-Minded Teamwork in Any Team*, your teammates will strive to achieve customer satisfaction while consistently achieving other business goals.

7 Mindfulness Training Lessons

Achieving Right-Minded Teamwork involves adopting an attitude of mindfulness. The *7 Mindfulness Training Lessons* teach you to think in a Right-Minded way, ensuring you **do no harm** as you **work as one** with your teammates.

These powerful lessons are summed up in one sentence, with emphasis on three words:

*Right-Minded Teammates **accept, forgive,** and **adjust** their thinking and work behavior.*

In every circumstance, especially during difficult team situations, Right-Minded Teammates practice mindfulness to move them from defensiveness and blame into a Right-Minded, allied way of thinking and behaving.

Inspired by *A Course in Miracles* and our Right Choice Model, the *7 Mindfulness Training Lessons* is a teaching tool designed to help those willing to apply them to ensure they return to the Unified Circle of Right-Minded Thinking.

Go to RightMindedTeamwork.com or visit your favorite book retailer to pick up your copy of *7 **Mindfulness Training Lessons**: Improve Teammates' Ability to Work as One with Right-Minded Thinking.*

10 Characteristics of Right-Minded Teammates

Right-Minded Teammates have many different surface traits and personalities. They are not all alike. They have numerous backgrounds, vastly different experiences, and a wide range of skills.

Nevertheless, it is understood that the Right-Minded Teammate, in their own particular behavioral style, happily live these characteristics because they align the teammate's authentic *self* with their team's version of the RMT motto: *do no harm, work as one,* and *none of us is as smart as all of us.*

You will find a complete description of these characteristics in RMT's book: ***Right-Minded Teamwork in Any Team:*** *The Ultimate Team Building Method to Create a Team That Works as One.*

1. Trust	2. Honesty	3. Tolerance
4. Gentleness	5. Joy	6. Defenselessness
7. Generosity	8. Patience	9. Open-Mindedness
	10. Faithfulness	

12 Steps Workshop Design Process

Design a Right-Minded, Team-Building Workshop:*12 Steps to Create a Team That Works as One.* This book will teach you how to design a practical, real-world team-building workshop.

The 12 steps are grouped into three phases: Contract, Commence, and Carry on. Written primarily for team facilitators, team leaders, and teammates can easily follow the steps to design a successful team-building workshop. Because this method engages teammates in designing the agenda, it virtually guarantees that teammates *cannot wait* to attend the workshop. They *know* that they will get real work done in a safe, "no harm" environment when they meet.

A Course in Miracles

Oneness. Forgiveness is the key to happiness, inner peace, undifferentiated unity, and ultimately – *oneness.* "A Course In Miracles (ACIM) is a unique spiritual self-study program designed to awaken us to the truth of our *oneness* with God and Love," as posted on ACIM.org and ACIM.org/ACIM/en. See the Foundation for A Course in Miracles at FACIM.org, where Ken Wapnick, the founder, created this beautiful definition.

A Course in Miracles is a psychological approach to spirituality where forgiveness is the central theme, and inner peace is the result.

ACIM and other moral and spiritual philosophies that advocate and help people everywhere **work together as One** has inspired Right-Minded Teamwork. We used Ken's definition as a guide to create the Right-Minded Teamwork definition.

Right-Minded Teamwork is a business-oriented, psychological approach to team building where acceptance, forgiveness, and adjustments are teammate characteristics and 100% customer satisfaction is the team's result.

All Right-Minded Teamwork methods, processes, and tools seamlessly work together to help you create and sustain a *Team That Works Together as **One**.*

Accept, Forgive, Adjust

These three terms are at the core of Right-Minded Teammate Attitudes & Behaviors. These verbs are also central to the *7 Mindfulness Training Lessons*, which are summed up in the sentence, *Right-Minded Teammates **accept**, **forgive**, and **adjust** their thinking and work behavior.*

Furthermore, these three concepts are included in the definition of Right-Minded Teamwork:

*Right-Minded Teamwork is a business-oriented, psychological approach to team building where **acceptance**, **forgiveness**, and **adjustment** are teammate characteristics, and 100% customer satisfaction is the team's result.*

Lastly, these terms are also incorporated as three of the five steps in the *Right Choice Model*, which describes accountable and responsible Right-Minded Teamwork behavior.

Ally or Adversary Teammate

Right-Minded Teamwork asserts that as teammates, you either work together as allies or pull apart, viewing each other as adversaries.

Allies work towards achieving team goals. Adversaries work towards individual elevation, which separates and divides the team.

To determine whether you are in an ally or adversary mindset, ask yourself, *Do I want to be right, or do I want our team to be successful?* Allies want to be part of a successful team. Adversaries want to be right, no matter the cost.

As an adversary, Ego persuades you to compete with your teammates. As an ally, Reason says the opposite. Reason gently reminds you that separateness prevents true success. There cannot be oneness or collaboration where there is competition.

As the Decision-Maker, you choose to follow either Reason or Ego. You either collaborate or compete. You are an ally or adversary. There is no middle ground.

If you choose to follow Reason and become an ally, you embrace and live your team's Work Agreements. If you decide to follow Ego, you become an adversary, creating a battleground inside yourself and your team.

To transform competitive adversaries into collaborative allies, start by following the *Right Choice Model*, creating team *Work Agreements*, and applying the *7 Mindfulness Training Lessons*.

Avoidance Behavior

Even though the term "avoidance behavior" is not often mentioned in the Right-Minded Teamwork model or books, avoidance behavior is easy to detect in teammates and RMT processes. If you notice it occurring, from an RMT perspective, you can consider it wrong-minded, adversarial behavior.

Identifying avoidance behaviors and attitudes and understanding the harm they cause is the first step in moving from a wrong-minded place into Right-Mindedness. The *7 Mindfulness Training Lessons* and the *Right Choice Model* are excellent tools for teaching yourself and your team how to act and behave in a Right-Minded, accountable way.

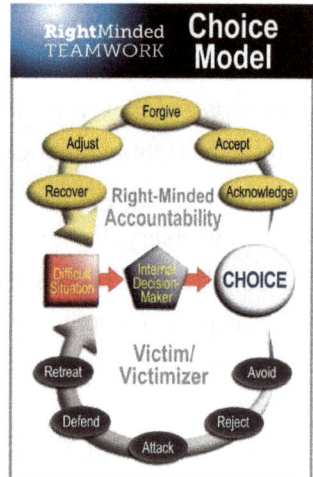

For example, if you look carefully at the *Right Choice Model's* lower loop, you will notice that the victim or victimizer first avoids the situation when a difficult situation occurs.

When Right-Minded Teammates ask themselves the *Right Choice Model* question, *How did I* **create**, **promote**, *or* **allow** *this difficult situation to happen?* they often realize they have unconsciously demonstrated avoidance behavior. Then, noticing their mistake, they simply choose to **accept**, **forgive**, and **adjust** their approach and return to living in accordance with their team *Work Agreements*.

Battleground:
Where People Are Punished for Mistakes

The battleground represents wrong-minded thinking. It is a mental attitude or thought system that defends and encourages adversarial behaviors such as blame and attack.

Think of the battleground as a psychological symbol for those moments when you realize you are listening to Ego, not Reason (like when you notice avoidance behavior). You recognize that you are having an Ego attack for whatever reason and have made a wrong-minded choice. When you are in the battleground, you "punish" others for their mistakes, either by victimizing others or becoming a victim yourself.

On the other hand, when you are in your right mind, you see your team as a lovely and safe classroom, the opposite of the battleground. You do not punish others. You choose, instead, to rise above the conflict.

The purpose of recognizing the battlegrounds in your mind is to own the pain that you are causing yourself which helps you recognize that you consciously want to leave it, overlook it, rise above it, and to transport your mind into the classroom where you return to the forgiving Unified Circle of Right-Minded Thinking with your teammates.

Right-Minded Teammates working in safe and supportive classrooms do not fight, blame, or punish. Instead, they choose oneness over separateness. They are committed to the team's success and achieving team goals.

To overcome a battleground in yourself or your team, go to RightMindedTeamwork.com, or visit your favorite book retailer to pick up your copy of **How to Apply the Right Choice Model**: *Create a Right-Minded Team That Works as One*. Inside, you will find a list of battleground attitudes and behaviors as well as the costs and benefits of classroom versus battleground thinking and behaving.

Certified Master Facilitator (CMF)

The Certified Master Facilitator (CMF) credential is a mark of excellence for facilitators. It is the highest available certification for facilitators. To learn more or to find a certified facilitator worldwide, visit the International Institute for Facilitation at INIFAC.org.

Classroom:
Where People Learn from Mistakes

Like the battleground, the classroom is a symbol. But unlike the battlefield, where people punish or are punished, the classroom is where you learn and find inspiration.

At some point in your past, you have experienced the joy and wonder of learning. Right-Minded Teamwork invites you to view your team as a safe place to experience this wonder and joy as you learn new teamwork skills and collaborate to achieve team goals.

When you are experiencing fear in any form or realize you are having an Ego attack, you are in the battleground. To return to the classroom, say to yourself, *There is nothing to fear. In my mind, I choose to rise above this silly battleground and head to my Right-Minded classroom. There, we are committed to do no harm and work as one. There, we will find solutions.*

By recognizing the fear behind your Ego attack and reminding yourself to return to the classroom, you experience a **moment of Reason**. You also strengthen your Right-Minded thought system and restore yourself to Right-Minded Thinking.

In the RMT book *How to Apply the Right Choice Model: Create a Right-Minded Team That Works as One,* you will find a list of 30 Right-Minded and wrong-minded attitudes and behaviors, plus the associated costs and benefits to your team.

Communication Work Agreement

What you think – *your thought system* – drives your communication in one of two ways. You either communicate as a collaborative ally or as a competitive, dysfunctional, and emotionally immature adversary.

Teams that work as one and achieve their goals regularly seek out opportunities to improve communication. They take positive action by creating and living a Communication Work Agreement that describes their team's agreed-upon communication style.

Right-Minded communication is a core concept in the book ***Right-Minded Teamwork****: 9 Right Choices for Building a Team That Works as One,* available at RightMindedTeamwork.com or your favorite book retailer.

To create your team's Communication Work Agreement, follow the suggestions in the book *How to Facilitate Teamwork Agreements: A Practical, 10-Step Process for Building a Right-Minded Team That Works as One.*

In there, you will find two real examples of which one is a team Communication Work Agreement.

Create, Promote, Allow

These three concepts form the foundation of the *Right Choice Model's* essential question:

*How have I **created**, **promoted**, or **allowed** this situation to occur?*

Asking and honestly answering this question ensures teammates are "owning their part" in a difficult situation.

These three concepts are also integrated into *7 Mindful Training Lessons: Improve Teammate's Ability to Work as One with Right-Minded Thinking.*

High-performing Right-Minded Teammates always ask themselves this question because it leads them to solutions. It is a clear demonstration of the RMT motto, "**Do no harm. Work as one.**"

Critical Few:
Complete Important Tasks First

When a team is stuck in the "full-plate syndrome," identifying and completing the critical few - those tasks that have the largest and most direct impact on the team's success - is key to moving forward.

At the root of the full-plate syndrome is the **team's collective fear**, driven by Ego, which declares you will get in trouble if you do not do it all... even though the truth is you can never do it all.

People who listen to Ego believe they do not have a choice. Rather than realistically prioritizing their workload, they punish themselves for failing to meet the unreasonable goal of completing everything. They drain their energy, lose their focus, and make mistakes. They become powerless, cynical, and burned out.

But Reason reminds us that we always have this choice:

We can either win by doing the critical few tasks, or we can lose by attempting to do everything.

Spend more time doing the right things right and let go of low-value tasks. Holding on to lower-value tasks is **not security**. It is **incarceration**.

The "critical few" concept is discussed in the book ***Right-Minded Teamwork***: *9 Right Choices for Building a Team That Works as One*.

See **Recognition: Make It Easy to Keep Going** for a related concept.

Decision-Maker: The Real You

Ken Wapnick, Ph.D., created the term "Decision-Maker" to define the "real you" in *A Course in Miracles*. For more on his work, visit FACIM.org.

Within Right-Minded Teamwork, the *Right Choice Model* uses the term "Decision-Maker" to describe the part of you that chooses to listen to and follow either the wrong-minded ways of Ego or the Right-Minded ways of Reason.

DECISION MAKER

Your Decision-Maker is 100% responsible for who you choose to follow, what you choose to think, and how you choose to behave.

Right-Mindedness is achieved when you listen to and follow Reason. Listening means calming your Ego mind, trusting your intuition, and allowing space for a **moment of Reason** to arise.

When Right-Mindedness becomes an integral part of a team, the team consistently works together as one, doing no harm, within the forgiving Unified Circle of Right-Minded Thinking. When teammates do that, they are demonstrating and extending Right-Minded Teamwork to everyone.

To learn more about Reason, Ego, and the Decision-Maker, pick up the book *Reason, Ego, & the Right-Minded Teamwork Myth: The Philosophy & Process for Creating a Right-Minded Team That Works Together as One.*

Decision-Maker: Trust Your Intuition

If thinking about Reason and Ego is new to you, it can be helpful to think of Reason as your positive intuition and Ego as your negative, arrogant, and sometimes vindictive intuition.

At different times throughout our lives, we all have listened to and followed each of these teachers.

Stop and remember when you had a hunch or a feeling as to what you should do or say in a particular situation. Did you ignore your intuition? Let's say you did not follow your instinct, and it turned out to be a mistake. What did you say to yourself and others?

I wish I had trusted my intuition!

As this memory illustrates, **you already know how to listen and be mindful** of your intuition. It is your natural, pre-separation state of mind [See **Oneness vs. Separateness**].

You just need to do it regularly.

Decision-Making Work Agreement

Every team needs a Decision-Making Work Agreement that clearly defines how decisions are made and who makes them. Creating a general agreement and putting it into your team's Operating System's Business Plan as a team Work Agreement makes good business sense.

If you do not currently have a Decision-Making team agreement or you have not updated it recently, I highly recommend you do that as soon as it is practical.

Incidentally, Decision-Making is #18 in the *Team Performance Factor Assessment* that you will use every 90 days to keep your team focused and on track. See **Team Operating System**.

In the book, ***How to Facilitate Team Work Agreements****: A Practical, 10-Step Process for Building a Right-Minded Team That Works as One,* you will find two real agreement examples. The first one is a behavioral team Communication Work Agreement, and the other is a Decision-Making Work Agreement. Check it out and use it as a model for your team's Decision-Making Work Agreement.

Desire & Willingness:
Preconditions for Accountability

Even though the terms "desire" and "willingness" are not often mentioned in Right-Minded Teamwork materials (except within the *Right Choice Model*), Right-Mindedness and accountability are virtually synonymous.

The concepts of desire and willingness permeate all RMT methods and processes simply because it is impossible to think in a Right-Minded way, behave with Right-Minded Accountability, and achieve Right-Minded Teamwork without a heartfelt desire and genuine willingness to do so.

The *Right Choice Model* found in the book ***How to Apply the Right Choice Model****: Create a Right-Minded Team That Works as One* teaches, *Right-Minded Accountability is the desire and willingness to change my mind and behavior in order to effectively respond to difficult team situations.*

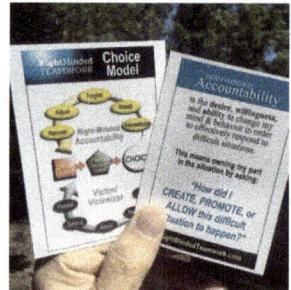

If you share the Right Choice Model with your team and distribute the Right Choice cards to teammates, you will see the definition of "desire and willingness" on the cards.

Do No Harm. Work as One.

The Right-Minded philosophy is founded on two universal truths:

Do No Harm.
Work As One.

None of us is as smart as all of us.
Right-Minded Teammates know that working collaboratively together, in a Right-Minded manner, is the only way to create the kind of teamwork that achieves and sustains 100% customer satisfaction. Said differently, these teammates genuinely want and need their fellow teammates.

Do no harm and work as one.
As a Right-Minded Teammate, you can be firm, direct, gentle, and compassionate, all at the same time. You do not blame yourself or others for mistakes. You and your teammates are allies, not adversaries, working together towards your shared goals.

Ego & Ego Attack

Ego is the negative, wrong-minded teacher who continually tells you how difficult the world is and how you must constantly fight to survive.

Reason is the opposite of Ego. Reason teaches you to *do unto others as you would have them do unto you.*

EGO

Ego believes everyone is out to get you and directs you to *do unto others before they do unto you.* Ego is also the creator of the tiny, mad idea of separation presented in the *Right-Minded Teamwork Myth.*

An Ego attack is a flash of negative, out-of-control emotion. It happens when you believe the awful feeling you are experiencing has been caused by something someone else said or did to you. Without thinking, you become behaviorally triggered; your body language, tone of voice, and the words you say become mean-spirited. An Ego attack is the opposite of a **moment of Reason**.

As soon as you realize you are experiencing an Ego attack, you must train your mind to say, *I am angry. I have lost control. I'm not upset for the reason I think. I am out of my right mind. I need a moment of Reason to gain control of my attitude. I must return to the classroom so I can find a Right-Minded way of replying that allows us to do no harm and work as one.*

Interlocking Accountability

Interlocking accountability is a crucial RMT concept that is primarily used in *How to Facilitate Team Work Agreements: a Practical, 10-Step Process for Building a Right-Minded Team That Works as One.*

When your team creates Work Agreements, it is highly recommended that one of your agreements includes an interlocking accountability statement so that teammates agree, ahead of time, how to compassionately confront a teammate who continues to break your Work Agreements.

Interlocking Accountability means many things, including:

- Giving positive reinforcement when someone continues to do a great job of living the Work Agreements.
- Confronting someone in a supportive and safe but firm way if they continue to break the spirit or letter of the team's Work Agreement.
- Being accountable to each other for achieving or accomplishing the desired outcome of the Work Agreements.
- Recovering and learning from mistakes rather than denying or punishing those who make mistakes. This strengthens team spirit and trust.
- Creating and sustaining teammate trust because teammates who believe everyone will live their part of the Work Agreement will create Right-Minded Teamwork.

Moment of Reason

When you are facing a challenge such as an Ego attack, and you experience a positive and perhaps surprising moment of revelation, clarity, or sanity, you have achieved a moment of Reason.

These moments occur when you genuinely try to move from the battleground into the classroom. When Reason's teaching breaks through, you move from wrong-mindedness into Right-Mindedness.

Moments of Reason are magnificent. They are a cornerstone of your Right-Minded thought system. When they happen, you feel confident and at peace. You know what you should do, what to say, and to whom.

In moments of Reason, you know beyond a shadow of a doubt that you want and need your teammates. You easily return to the Unified Circle of Right-Minded Thinking, where teammates forgive one another, do no harm, and work as one.

Onboarding New Teammates

When a new leader or teammate joins your team, it is vitally important to properly onboard them within their first week on the job. In a single short meeting where everyone attends, the onboarding is easily and effectively accomplished.

Present all your RMT goals and Work Agreements along with why they were created. They ask you clarifying questions. Afterward, you ask them to accept the team's goals and actively live the team's Work Agreements.

Oneness vs. Separateness

Oneness is a psychological state of mind. It can be described in many ways using phrases such as *None of us is as smart as all of us,* or *do no harm,* and *work as one.*

Separateness is the opposite of oneness. To become a Right-Minded teammate, you must train your mind to choose attitudes and behaviors that create and extend oneness, not project separateness.

For a list of 30 examples of oneness, see the Right-Minded Teamwork Attitudes & Behaviors list found in numerous RMT books.

The concepts and story behind oneness and separateness are introduced in RMT's book, **Reason, Ego & the Right-Minded Teamwork Myth:** *The Philosophy and Process for Creating a Right-Minded Team That Works Together as One.*

In this book, you will learn about Ego's "tiny, mad idea" of wanting more "stuff" and how Ego's choices led us all into a world of separation. That tiny, mad moment was, literally, the **birth of separation**. But, as the Myth reveals, Reason is always ready to lead us back into oneness - our pre-separation state – joyfully described as the Unified Circle of Right-Minded Thinking where we can do no harm and work as one.

Preventions & Interventions

In RMT's **Design a Right-Minded, Team-Building Workshop:** *12 Steps to Create a Team That Works as One*, the team-building facilitator and team leader meet early on to proactively identify potential issues that could keep teammates from achieving the workshop's desired outcomes.

This discussion leads to creating *preventions* that the team leader or facilitator takes to help prevent those issues from happening. The facilitator and team leader also agree on how to intervene in case the preventions don't work. Much of the time, however, preventions do their job and make *interventions* during team-building workshops unnecessary.

To learn more about effective preventions and interventions, go to RightMindedTeamwork.com or your favorite book retailer, and pick up your copy of these two books:

How to Facilitate Team Work Agreements: *A Practical, 10-Step Process for Building a Right-Minded Team That Works as One*

Design a Right-Minded, Team-Building Workshop: *12 Steps to Create a Team That Works as One*

Psychological Goals

A team's psychological goals describe how teammates intentionally choose to think and behave as they work together to achieve their team's business goals.

Psychological goals, such as achieving mutual trust and respect among teammates, may be viewed as a team's collective school of thought, values, or thought system.

These consciously chosen goals, captured in team Work Agreements, clarify the team's principles or standards of behavior.

Here is a specific example of a psychological goal you will find in several RMT materials:

> *When difficult team situations happen, we accept, forgive, and adjust our attitudes and behavior. We always find solutions because we believe that none of us is as smart as all of us.*

Reason

Reason is a mythological character and symbolic guide who shows you how to think and behave in a Right-Minded way. As your Right-Minded teacher, Reason helps you differentiate and choose between Right-Minded and wrong-minded attitudes and behaviors.

REASON

Reason is the opposite of Ego. Whereas Ego believes everyone is out to get you and instructs you to *do unto others before they do unto you,* Reason teaches you to *do unto others as you would have them do unto you.*

Ego encourages and projects separateness.
Reason cultivates and extends oneness.

Reason is that part of your mind that always speaks for the Right Choice attitudes and behaviors. When you need a **moment of Reason** to find the best way to respond to a difficult team situation, say to yourself

I am here to be truly helpful.

I am here to represent Reason who sent me.

I do not have to worry about what to say or what to do because Reason who sent me will direct me.

When you experience a moment of Reason (a moment of revelation, clarity, or sanity regarding a particular challenge), "remembering" Reason's gentle guidance towards oneness restores your mind to the forgiving Unified Circle of Right-Minded Thinking.

For the full story of Ego's tiny, mad idea of separation and how Reason waits even today to bring us back to oneness, pick up your copy of the book *Reason, Ego & the Right-Minded Teamwork Myth: The Philosophy and Process for Creating a Right-Minded Team That Works Together as One.*

Reason, Ego & the Right-Minded Teamwork Myth

This book teaches two significant concepts:

- the Right-Minded Teamwork Myth is a short tale that presents RMT's underlying teamwork philosophy of doing no harm and working as one
- the Right-Minded Teamwork team-building tools, methods, and processes to create Right-Minded, productive teams.

The RMT Myth is a short, simple story. It follows three characters: Reason, Ego, and you, the Decision-Maker. Simply put, the RMT Myth and philosophy advocate for teammates to follow Reason's path of oneness instead of following Ego's disastrous advice to seek separateness and prioritize selfishness.

Following the RMT Myth, you will learn about the Right-Minded Teamwork process. Unlike the story, the RMT process is no myth. It is practical, deliberate, and reliable.

The RMT process is a set of interconnected, team-building methods that together form a self-perpetuating, continuous improvement system. This process allows you to integrate the aspirations of the RMT Myth into your team in a way that helps you achieve your business goals.

This book teaches the RMT process and provides a clear overview of the seven other RMT team-building books that, when used together, form a continuous improvement process guaranteed to support team growth and success.

Recognition:
Make It Easy to Keep Going

Authentic recognition is not about bestowing company shirts and prizes. It is about giving and receiving genuine appreciation for a job well done.

Recognition plays a critical role in growing your team's business because it keeps your team's spirit ignited. Unfortunately, many people work in team environments where there is little to no recognition. These teammates are discouraged. They do not give their best to the team. Why should they?

Discouraged teammates are like racehorses. If a horse is giving you only 80%, you can whip him, and he will give you 90%. Whip him again, and he will give you 100%. But if you whip him again, after he has already given you everything he has, he will drop back to 80%, or maybe even less. He has learned that you are going to whip him regardless, even if he works harder. So why should he give you his best?

Whipped people leave teams.

Far too often, the ones who leave are the most talented teammates. People who receive legitimate and genuine recognition stay and contribute. Shirts and prizes cannot earn that kind of loyalty or effort.

In the book *Right-Minded Teamwork: 9 Right Choices for Building a Team That Works as One*, you will learn that Recognition is one of the 9 Right Choices.

See **Critical Few: Complete Important Tasks First**. for a related concept.

Right Choice Model

The *Right Choice Model* is an effective teaching aid that will help you and your teammates choose your own set of unique, "right" teamwork attitudes and behaviors.

Inspired by *A Course in Miracles, The Right Choice Model* consists of two circles. The upper loop of acceptance, forgiveness, and adjustment represents the Unified Circle of Right-Minded Thinking.

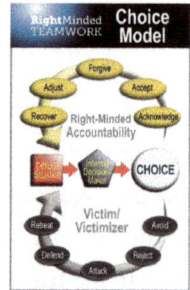

The lower loop of rejection, Ego attack, and defensiveness describes the separated or divided circle of wrong-minded thinking.

To learn more about this simple but powerful teaching model, go to RightMindedTeamwork.com or your favorite book retailer, and pick up your copy of *How to Apply the Right Choice Model: Create a Right-Minded Team That Works as One*.

Right-Minded Teamwork's 5-Element Framework

Right-Minded Teamwork is a business-oriented, psychological approach to team building where acceptance, forgiveness, and adjustment are teammate characteristics, and 100% customer satisfaction is the team's result.

Right-Minded Teamwork is built off a framework of 5 Elements consisting of two goals and three teamwork methods.

1. Team **Business Goal**: Achieve 100% Customer Satisfaction
2. Team **Psychological Goal**: Commit to Right-Minded Thinking
3. Team **Work Agreements**: Create & Follow Commitments
4. **Team Operating System**: Make It Effective & Efficient
5. **Right-Minded Teammates**: Strengthen Individual Performance

To learn more, go to RightMindedTeamwork.com or your favorite book retailer, and pick up your copy of *Right-Minded Teamwork in Any Team: The Ultimate Team-Building Method to Create a Team That Works as One.*

236 · DAN HOGAN

Right-Minded Teamwork's 5 Element Implementation Plan

There is no one right way to implement RMT's 5 Elements but the three-workshop plan presented in the book *Right-Minded Teamwork in Any Team: The Ultimate Team-Building Method to Create a Team That Works as One* has proven effective countless times.

Here's a brief overview.

First Workshop
Create **psychological goals** plus at least one **Work Agreement**.

Second Workshop
Reaffirm **business goals** and agree on a **team operating system**.

Third Workshop
Encourage and support Right-Minded **Teammate development**.

After the third workshop, and every 90 days after that, you will apply RMT's *Team Operating System & Performance Factor Assessment* to identify opportunities, take action, and achieve new teamwork improvements.

Right-Minded Teamwork
Attitudes & Behaviors

The Right-Minded Teamwork model includes a list of 30 behavioral and process-oriented teammate attitudes and behaviors with their associated costs and benefits. I collected and compiled these over three decades of team-building workshops.

This valuable list includes clear, specific, right, and wrong behaviors "taught" to us by either Reason or Ego.

Thoughts and attitudes always precede teamwork behavior. Right-Minded attitudes come from Reason. Wrong-minded attitudes come from Ego.

The good news is that Right-Minded attitudes are natural. They are already inside you and your teammates. When you think about any of the wrong-minded Ego attitudes listed you will see in the list, ask yourself,

> *Was I born with these depressing, debilitating, and awful attitudes?*

Your answer will always be **"no!"** You learned those wrong-minded attitudes from Ego. That means *you can unlearn them, too*.

You can find the list in several RMT books, including *How to Apply the Right Choice Model: Create a Right-Minded Team That Works as One*, available at RightMindedTeamwork.com or your favorite book retailer.

238 · DAN HOGAN

Right-Mindedness vs. Wrong-Mindedness

"Mindedness" is what you choose to think and perceive. Right-Mindedness refers to the positive mental state, perceptions, choices, and actions you demonstrate when following Reason's guidance.

Wrong-mindedness refers to the negative mental state that occurs when you follow Ego's advice.

> *Mindfulness is a journey without distance to a goal **you want to achieve**.*

In the book ***How to Apply the Right Choice Model***: *Create a Right-Minded Team That Works as One*, you will find a list of rewards and consequences for choosing Right-Mindedness.

In the book ***7 Mindfulness Training Lessons***: *Improve Teammates' Ability to Work as One with Right-Minded Thinking*, you will learn that in every circumstance, and especially during difficult team situations, Right-Minded Teammates practice mindfulness, or Right-Mindedness, to move them into an ally-focused way of thinking and behaving.

Both of these books will help you accept that your mind is split between two thought systems. At one moment, you are following Reason, and the next, Ego. It is impossible to create and sustain Right-Minded Thinking with a split mind. To heal your split mind, you want to apply the *7 Mindful Training Lessons* and the *Right Choice Model's* attitudes and behaviors.

To bring your team back into the forgiving Unified Circle of Right-Minded Thinking, pick up your copy of these books at your favorite book retailer or RightMindedTeamwork.com.

RMT Facilitator

The RMT Facilitator has a special function. Simply put, their expert facilitation *transforms* well-meaning dysfunctional souls into *healthy and functional teammates*.

Using the array of RMT tools, the RMT Facilitator guides teammates in converting their team mistakes into *do-no-harm-work-as-one* attitudes and behaviors.

Teammates are perpetually grateful for the RMT facilitator's help in achieving and sustaining Right-Minded Teamwork. Some even say their RMT Facilitator *saved them*. Team leaders and teammates continually seek the RMT Facilitator's support for years to come.

Team transformations are the RMT Facilitator's **special function**.

Team Management System:
An RMT's Enterprise-Wide Process

An enterprise's Team Management System (TMS) aligns all teammates' attitudes and work behavior throughout the organization. An effective TMS ensures everyone is doing their part to help the organization achieve the enterprise's vision, mission, and strategic goals.

RMT's Team Management System involves integrating RMT's 5-Element Framework into all teams.

1. Team **Business Goal**: Achieve 100% Customer Satisfaction
2. Team **Psychological Goal**: Commit to Right-Minded Thinking
3. Team **Work Agreements**: Create & Follow Commitments
4. **Team Operating System**: Make It Effective & Efficient
5. **Right-Minded Teammates**: Strengthen Individual Performance

To learn more, go to RightMindedTeamwork.com or your favorite book retailer, and purchase your copy of *Achieve Your Organization's Strategic Plan: Create a Right-Minded, Team Management System to Ensure All Teams Work as One.*

Team Operating System & Performance Factor Assessment

RMT's Team Operating System is a six-step, 90-day, continuous improvement operating system that organizes your team functions to increase the likelihood of achieving customer satisfaction.

The system also includes the *Team Performance Factor Assessment* [step 3], which you will use to help teammates identify two to three improvement opportunities every 90 days.

The 25 performance factors in this assessment are aligned with and thus measure the six steps of RMT's Team Operating System. They effectively measure all aspects of Right-Minded Teamwork.

If you want your team to operate more effectively and efficiently, apply this 90-day process after your team has completed the first three RMT workshops. For a brief explanation, see the glossary: *Right-Minded Teamwork's 5 Element Implementation Plan.*

Apply the three-workshop plan and the operating system, and you nearly guarantee your team will create Right-Minded Teamwork.

To learn the process, go to RightMindedTeamwork.com or your favorite book retailer, and pick up your copy of ***Right-Minded Teamwork in Any Team:*** *The Ultimate Team-Building Method to Create a Team That Works as One.*

Thought System

<u>What you believe *is* your thought system</u>. Pause and reflect on this truth, and above all, be thankful that it is true.

Whether you are consciously aware of it or not, your thought system is the lens through which you view the world. Without exception, everyone has one. And though there are many variations, there are *only two thought systems* from which to choose:

- A Right-Minded thought system, which extends ally beliefs of acceptance, forgiveness, and adjustment to everyone, everywhere, forever
- A wrong-minded system, which projects adversarial assaults of rejection, attack, and defensiveness to everyone, everywhere, forever

Once you have developed a thought system of any kind, you live it and teach it. Even if you are not entirely aware of it, it remains at the forefront of your mind, influencing your daily behaviors and choices.

If your thought system is negative, or you choose to follow Ego into an unnecessary and adversarial competition, you cannot be a happy, successful teammate.

To live in the land of oneness where your workplace is a safe and supportive classroom and where you and your teammates work as one to achieve team goals, you must train your mind and align your thought system with the teachings of Reason.

There is no possible compromise between these two thought systems. You either collaborate, or you compete. When you follow Ego, you take your team to the battleground. When you choose to follow Reason, you willingly create and genuinely strive to live your team's Work Agreements. With Reason's help, you transform your team into a lovely, collaborative, successful classroom.

The choice is clear.

Reject Ego. Embrace Reason.

Be Thankful.

Train Your Mind

When your mind is well-trained in Reason's Decision-Making ways, Ego attacks do not throw you off course. When a difficult team situation happens, you immediately stop for a **moment of Reason**. You refocus on oneness, rise above the battleground, and remember to live your Work Agreements in your classroom.

To train your mind simply means practicing your team's Work Agreements, which represent your psychological goals, as often as possible, especially during difficult team situations.

Uncovering Root Cause

The Right-Minded Teamwork philosophy advocates leaders, teammates, and facilitators resolve the root cause of teamwork issues instead of making the mistake of addressing symptoms.

Though this view is discussed in many RMT materials, uncovering the root cause is heavily emphasized as a core concept in the book *Design a Right-Minded, Team-Building Workshop: 12 Steps to Create a Team That Works as One.*

Inside that book, you will find a story about a well-meaning team leader who asked me, as their team-building facilitator, if I could teach a three-day workshop in just two days. He believed a quick team event would address the problem he saw in his team.

But the problem he was seeing was only the symptom, not the root cause of the issue. Had I agreed and given him what he asked for, the team would still be struggling with the same issue. And, as a facilitator, I would have failed both the team and the leader.

Instead, by pausing to look for the root cause of the team challenge first, we ended up designing and executing a practical, Right-Minded Teamwork workshop to solve the actual underlying problem.

By seeking out the root cause first, we delivered the leader's desired result, even though the workshop we held was not what he had initially asked for.

To improve your ability to uncover root causes and read this short story, go to your favorite book retailer or RightMindedTeamwork.com and pick up your copy of *Design a Right-Minded, Team-Building Workshop: 12 Steps to Create a Team That Works as One.*

Unified Circle of Right-Minded Thinking

When your team discusses and agrees on your psychological goals – your consciously chosen set of attitudes and behaviors as described in your Work Agreements – you have created your team's collective thought system.

By uniting with each other in this way and openly committing to one another through your Work Agreements, you are renouncing Ego in yourself and your teammates and collectively committing to train your minds to follow Reason.

This process of creating team Work Agreements is your undivided declaration of interdependence. Your assertion is saying,

> *We hold these mindful truths to be self-evident that all minds are created equal, and whosoever believes that will have everlasting freedom to choose Right-Minded Teamwork.*

Your declaration plus your daily acts of living your team Work Agreements *is your return* to the forgiving Unified Circle of Right-Minded Thinking.

Work Agreements

A Work Agreement is a collective promise made by teammates to transform non-productive, adversarial behavior into collaborative teamwork behavior. Work Agreements are a key tool for teammates and teams who aspire to do no harm and work as one.

Work Agreements are not flimsy ground rules. They are emotionally mature work performance commitments. Work Agreements announce your dedication to oneness and demonstrate your inner belief that *none of us is as smart as all of us.*

Your team's collective Work Agreements also define your team's psychological goals and thought system. They ensure you conduct your day-to-day work from within your team's Unified Circle of Right-Minded Thinking.

To learn more about the power of Work Agreements and how to use them to transform your team, go to RightMindedTeamwork.com or your favorite book retailer, and pick up your copy of **How to Facilitate Team Work Agreements**: *A Practical, 10-Step Process for Building a Right-Minded Team That Works as One.*

Resources

To download RMT models and processes to give teammates, go to RightMindedTeamwork.com, and search for this book's companion *Reusable Resources & Templates*.

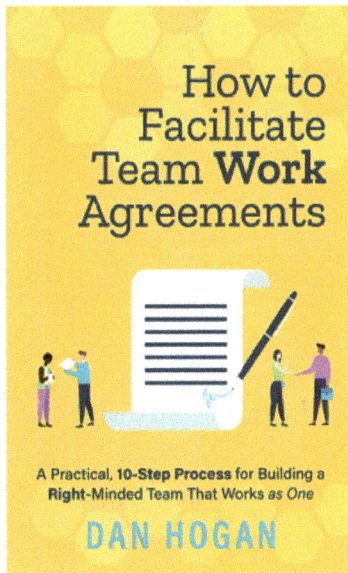

14 Characteristics of a Successful Team Building Facilitator

Friendly	Gentle	Playful
Collaborative	Outcome-Driven	Engaging
Attentive	Helpful	Non-Judgmental
Facilitative	Practical	Self-Reflecting
Focused	Mature	

Every facilitator brings their own personality and flair to their facilitation work, but successful facilitators share some key characteristics.

Friendly

The facilitator sets the tone for the workshop. When teammates walk in feeling welcomed and excited to be there, the facilitator has played a key role in creating that atmosphere. With the best facilitators, you feel like you're being welcomed into their home.

Collaborative

Facilitators use their body language, tone of voice, and word choice to support workshop outcomes. They also use their environment strategically.

By setting the tone and carefully arranging the room, facilitators can create a professional yet comfortable atmosphere that encourages real discussion amongst all teammates. This air of active involvement creates a collaborative learning environment.

Attentive

An effective facilitator continually practices seeing, hearing, and feeling the interpersonal dynamics in the room. They watch body language and listen to the tone of voice, looking for patterns. They also observe how listeners react to other speakers' information.

Facilitative

It may sound obvious, but good facilitators know how to use facilitative tools. They realize using these tools is the "means" and not the "end," so they do not overuse them. Rather than attempting to facilitate the process perfectly, they maintain focus on achieving the meeting outcome(s).

Focused

Excellent facilitators stay one mental step ahead of participants. They continually ask themselves, "What's next on the agenda?" and "How will we get from here to the desired outcome and beyond?" They bring strategic thinking and strategic facilitation into their workshops.

Gentle

When there's tension or conflict in the room, effective facilitators don't avoid the problem. Instead, they gently move towards it. They "do no harm" to everyone.

They look at the choices being made by participants. They listen for key points and reflect them back. They are skilled at summarizing. They know how to carefully reflect a situation so participants can see the problem clearly and recognize the necessity for addressing it.

Outcome-Driven

Strong facilitators use the workshop agenda, particularly the meeting's desired outcome, to keep the discussions on track. They keep the outcome firmly implanted in their minds, and they use it as a filter to screen teammate communication.

They constantly ask themselves how the current discussion relates to the overall desired outcome. If it relates, they stay out of the way and let the participants do their work. If the conversation goes off track, they interrupt and ask, "How does this information help achieve our desired outcome?"

Helpful

Instead of asking people to accept the meeting's desired outcomes blindly, good facilitators help participants identify "what's in it for them." Then, they synergize the teammates' motivations to align with the desired meeting outcomes. For important meetings, this work is done before the meeting, not during.

Practical

Successful facilitators know there are two kinds of barriers: processes and people. While planning an important meeting, successful facilitators proactively ask themselves what could go wrong. They identify specific barriers within the team, and they plan ways to prevent these barriers from arising. They also plan how they will intervene if their preventions don't work.

Mature

The most effective facilitators are true to themselves. They know there is no one right way to facilitate. They don't try to mimic other successful facilitators; they find their own voice. They improve and grow their personal facilitation style.

Playful

Facilitators may be humorous, but they never use humor at anyone's expense.

Engaging

Good facilitators look for and take advantage of opportunities to get participants moving. Often, this means getting participants to do something with their entire bodies, not just their minds.

Non-Judgmental

Effective facilitators don't have to be neutral. But they do have to be willing to step aside from their own beliefs and values in order to facilitate objectively. They know how to share their opinions without directing, and regardless of their views, they offer their critical-thinking skills to help the group make the best decision.

Self-Reflecting

Successful facilitators ask themselves these honest questions:

- Do I understand the outcome from the stakeholders' perspectives?
- Have I done my homework, and am I prepared for the unexpected?
- If people get upset or things seem to go wrong in the meeting, do I have a predetermined set of values and principles to guide my choices and interactions?

When a facilitator can answer yes to these questions, they know they're ready.

Meeting Plan Checklist

Purpose of the Meeting _____
Desired Outcomes
    1. ABC
    2. XYZ

Stakeholders:

- Participants in meeting: What's in it for them?
- Non-participants: What's in it for them?
- What do participants need to do to prepare?

Decision-making method & fallback _____

Barriers to this meeting

- Processes Barriers
- People Barriers

Preventions & Interventions to the Barriers _____

Roles & Responsibilities

- Facilitator: _____
- Scribe: _____
- Timekeeper: _____
- Sponsors: _____
- Others: _____

Room Arrangement & other logistics_____
Meeting Notes & Distribution _____
Follow-up Strategies & Action Items _____

Team Workshop Agenda & Punch List

I created this Agenda and Punch List for a team during Step 9 of the 12-step Team-Building Workshop Design Process.

Purpose: To create and sustain a higher-performing team

Desired Outcomes

1. Discuss and agree on how to **improve meeting effectiveness**.

2. Discuss and agree on how to improve **team communications**.

3. Discuss and agree on how to improve **work ethics** so as to increase openness, trust, respect, and efficiency in our team.

4. Agree on how and when to address **customer satisfaction** and **roles & responsibilities.**

Agenda

1. **Welcome & Kick-Off**
   - Purpose, Desired Outcome
   - Review agenda, meeting behaviors & agreements

2. **Meeting Effectiveness & Communications**
   - Discuss and agree on how to improve
   - Solve the problem / create a Work Agreement

3. **First Punch List Topic**
   - Define the problem
   - Solve the problem / create a Work Agreement

4. **Second Punch List Topic**
   - Define the problem
   - Solve the problem / create a Work Agreement

5. **Tracking Performance**
   - Discuss and agree on how the team will track performance

6. **Close**
   - Agree on how / when to resolve the other Punch List topics
   - Wrap up…how was the meeting? (plus / delta)
   - Agreements and / or Action Plan review & commitment
   - Acknowledgements & appreciations

Punch List

This is a final Punch List (Step 8 of RMT's 12-Step Workshop Design Process) from a real RMT workshop Dan Hogan facilitated. A first draft would not have this much detail.

The Punch List is a summary of teammate interviews (Step 7 of RMT's 12-Step Workshop Design Process). If two or more teammates brought up a topic, issue, challenge and/or conflict in the facilitator interviews, the essence was captured in a question format.

A. Meeting Effectiveness & Communication

1. Many people said they want open, honest, and straightforward communication; what does that look like?
2. Is it OK to use toxic / inflammatory words, tone or body language? When you slip and use toxic communication, and you realize you wish you had not, what should you do? What is an appropriate apology?
3. If someone approaches you about their difficulty with your communication style, what should you do?
4. If someone comes to you and complains about another team member / leader, what should you do? If you continue to hear the same basic complaints from the same people, what should you do?

B. Work Ethic

This is about – interaction style, conflict resolution, work quality, productivity, interdependency, etc. - that increases trust, respect, and confidence in one another.

1. Is it OK to have an unresolved conflict if it affects individual and / or team productivity? If not, what is our work agreement regarding solving conflicts and / or giving performance feedback? For instance...
2. If someone doesn't do what they said they'd do (or are assigned to do) how do you call it out in a supportive way? How do you hold them accountable?
3. If a teammate doesn't perform like you believe they should, what should you do? For instance, if you believe another person should perform a particular responsibility, is it OK to call it out?
4. Trust & respect...if you do not trust another person and it affects your performance, what should you do?
5. If we feel we are not getting acknowledged / recognized for our work, what should we do?

C. Customer Satisfaction

1. Are we giving our customers both internal and external exceptional service?
2. Do we know for certain our customers believe we're giving them exceptional service? If yes, how? If no, why not?
3. Do we listen to our customers and give them what they need? If we do, then they are very excited about paying our department's budget – right?
4. Do our customers know our capabilities as well as we do? If no, why not? How do we / should we educate our customers?

D. Roles & Responsibilities

1. Who in our team is primarily responsible for customer relations and satisfaction? How do they ensure we are creating and sustaining an incredibly good relationship with them?

2. For those who have key responsibilities, what are the 3-5 key behaviors and / or results they need to demonstrate for our team? What support do they need from others in our department?

3. When you ask to perform a particular task, and you do not understand, agree with or feel it is your role and responsibility, what should you do? How should you question it?

4. Is everyone clear and in agreement with how decisions are made in our team?

5. Where are duplicate work efforts and how can we streamline those work processes?

Sample Agenda Template

	Name of Meeting Date: Time: Location:
Attendees	
Please Read	
Please Bring	

Purpose & Desired Outcomes

Purpose:

To determine:

- Who we are
- Where we're going
- How we're going to get there

Desired Outcomes:

1. Discuss and agree on ....
2. Develop a clear understanding of ....

Agenda		
What	Who	When
1. Kick-off: present, clarify and agree on the meeting's purpose and desired outcome	All	10 min
2.		
3.		
4. Closure: Review Action items & commit Meeting effectiveness – what we did well or need to improve Acknowledgments & appreciations		10-15 min

Report of Improvement Template

Our Goal or Outcome	

Information
   Start Date
   End Date
   Team Leader
   Teammates	

What Was Done	

Actual Improvement or Results
   Measurable
   Non-Measurable	

Cost of Improvement
   Measurable
   Non-Measurable	

Suggestions for Future Projects or Outcomes	
Acknowledgment of Contributions	

Top 10 To-Do's for Facilitating Successful Meetings

1. Purpose
Determine the Purpose of the meeting. Is it an information share, decision-making, updating/status meeting, innovation or creative problem identification, and problem-solving meeting?

2. Desired Outcomes
When the Purpose is clear, determine the meeting's Desired Outcomes. Your outcomes are products or results that are achieved by the end of the session. They are usually a list, a plan, a decision, an understanding, or a work agreement.

3. Agenda
The facilitator will create an agenda and will distribute it to all participants before the meeting. Teammates need to come prepared for the workshop. At a minimum, they need to think about and be prepared to offer solutions for achieving the workshop's desired outcomes.

It's also possible for routine meetings to develop the next meeting's agenda at the end of the previous meeting, thus saving time, which will ensure clarity, alignment, and accountability.

Start on time. End on time.

4. Attendees
The best way to determine who attends the meeting is to ask who is involved or affected by the meeting's Purpose and Desired Outcomes. Those are the people who should attend this meeting.

5. Decisions

If it's a decision-making meeting, then determine the decision-making and fall-back agreement. The decision-making agreement must be understood and accepted by all teammates at the beginning of the meeting.

6. Conduct

Participants will agree on their meeting conduct. At the beginning of the session, teammates will create ground rules or codes of conduct. Everyone agrees to abide by them.

The facilitator and teammates keep the meeting focused on achieving outcomes, not personalities. Deal with distractions; don't ignore them. Encourage people not to ramble; get to the point.

7. Roles

Define roles & responsibilities for the facilitator, scribe, leader, and teammate. A "role" could be that teammates will let the facilitator manage the conversation. A "responsibility" could be how to capture and disseminate meeting notes.

8. Facilitator

Meeting participants must allow the facilitator to traffic the conversation and allow them to intervene if the group's discussion deviates from the Desired Outcomes.

The facilitator and participants must use the meeting agreements to hold others accountable for predetermined behaviors. In essence, everyone is responsible for achieving the Desired Outcomes.

Statement capture: either the facilitator or scribe must capture meeting notes for the future.

9. Closure

The close should include an action item review that identifies owners and timelines for teams who conduct routine meetings.

Teams should conduct a short plus/delta that identifies proper and not-so-good meeting management. Every team must train itself to be more meeting efficient.

10. Accountability

All participants are accountable for creating a successful meeting.

If participants feel the meetings are not valuable, not well run, not well attended, not full of engagement, and they do NOT speak up, they are equally accountable for the poor performance. It is recommended that the leader intervene and have a "straight talk" session with all those involved.

The End

On behalf of **Reason** and all the **Right-Minded Teammate Decision-Makers**, we extend our best wishes to you and your teammates as you create another ***Right-Minded Team that Works Together as One***.

DECISION MAKER   REASON